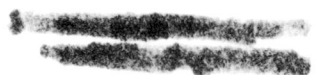

RECENT RESEARCHES IN THE MUSIC OF THE BAROQUE ERA, 159

Francesco Scarlatti

Six Concerti Grossi

Edited by Mark Kroll

A-R Editions, Inc.
Middleton, Wisconsin

For Gordon Dixon and the Avison Ensemble

Performance parts are available from the publisher.

A-R Editions, Inc., Middleton, Wisconsin
© 2010 by A-R Editions, Inc.

All rights reserved. No part of this book may be reproduced or transmitted in any form by any electronic or mechanical means (including photocopying, recording, or information storage and retrieval) without permission in writing from the publisher.

The purchase of this edition does not convey the right to perform it in public, nor to make a recording of it for any purpose. Such permission must be obtained in advance from the publisher.

A-R Editions is pleased to support scholars and performers in their use of *Recent Researches* material for study or performance. Subscribers to any of the *Recent Researches* series, as well as patrons of subscribing institutions, are invited to apply for information about our "Copyright Sharing Policy."

Printed in the United States of America

ISBN-13: 978-0-89579-669-1
ISBN-10: 0-89579-669-4
ISSN: 0484-0828

♾ The paper used in this publication meets the minimum requirements of the American National Standard for Information Sciences—Permanence of Paper for Printed Library Materials, ANSI Z39.48-1992.

Contents

Acknowledgments   vii

Introduction   ix

   Historical Background   ix
   Francesco (Antonio Nicola) Scarlatti   ix
   The Music of the Edition   x
   Notes on Performance   xi
   Notes   xii

Plates   xv

Concerto No. 1 in E Major

   I. Allegro   1
   II. [Allegro]   3
   III. Largo; [Allegro]   8
   IV. Affettuoso   13

Concerto No. 2 in C Minor

   I. [Largo]   17
   II. Andante   18
   III. Grave   21
   IV. [Allegro]   21

Concerto No. 3 in A Minor

   I. Allegro   26
   II. Andante   27
   III. [Larghetto]   30
   IV. [Allegro]   31

Concerto No. 4 in E Minor

   I. Largo; Andante   35
   II. Allegro   37
   III. Largo   40
   IV. [Allegro]   42

Concerto No. 8 in F Major

   I. Allegro   45
   II. Largo; [Allegro]   46
   III. Larghetto   51
   IV. Allegro   53

Concerto No. 9 in D Major

   I. Grave; Presto; Largo; Presto; Largo   57
   II. Larghetto   61
   III. Largo   66
   IV. Presto   68

Critical Report 73
    Sources 73
    Editorial Methods 73
    Critical Notes 75
    Notes 76

Acknowledgments

I express my sincere gratitude to Gordon Dixon, director of the Avison Ensemble of Newcastle upon Tyne and founder of the Charles Avison Society, for providing access to the workbooks of Avison, in which the music of this edition is found. Gordon invited me to come to Newcastle to study, perform, and edit the material in these workbooks shortly after they were discovered, and he later arranged for copies of the manuscripts to be sent to me. He has also asked me to provide material for the Avison Ensemble's ongoing series of recordings and performances of the repertoire from these books, and he continues to offer assistance and information. I am equally grateful to Ellen Golde, who played a significant role in the project by introducing me to Gordon and the people who support his efforts, helping to arrange my initial performance and research visits to Newcastle, and serving as a vital communication link between myself and the Avison Ensemble. I express my thanks for the generous assistance of the staff of the Newcastle City Library, Local Studies Collection, where the workbooks are housed. My appreciation also goes to Professors Wendy Heller and Carol Lieberman. They both read the introductory material for this edition, and their excellent comments and suggestions improved the final product immeasurably.

Introduction

Historical Background

England has often provided fertile soil for the transplantation of continental musicians and musical styles. The visit of Spanish organist Antonio de Cabezón in the mid-sixteenth century, for example, inspired an entire generation of English virginal composers. French art and music were briefly in favor after Charles II returned to the English throne from exile in France in 1660.[1] But the dominant musical influence in the British Isles during the last decades of the seventeenth century and throughout much of the eighteenth was Italian. A number of circumstances contributed to this development. One factor was the increasing number of English gentlemen and their families who took the Grand Tour to Italy and returned home with an enduring love of all things Italian, including music.[2] Italian musicians also began to immigrate to England during this time. Yet perhaps the most important musical event that tipped the scales in favor of the Italian style was the publication in England of the sonatas and concertos of Arcangelo Corelli (1653–1713). Roger North described these developments succinctly in 1728:

> There were 2 circumstances which concurred to convert English Musick intirely over from the French to the Italian taste. One was the coming over of ... Nichola Matteis; he was a sort of precursor who made way for what was to follow.... Then came over Corellys first consort that cleared the ground of all other sorts of musick whatsoever; by degrees the rest of his consorts & at last the conciertos came, all which are to the musitians like the bread of life.[3]

The Italian concerto grosso of Corelli and his followers was particularly significant. It established the model for all works in the genre that followed and created a devoted following in an entire generation of British musicians, chief among them Charles Avison (1709–70) of Newcastle.[4] The concerto grosso would in fact enjoy enduring influence and popularity in England well into the latter years of the eighteenth century. As Charles Burney described the situation in 1789, "The *Concertos* of Corelli seem to have withstood all the attacks of time and fashion.... They preclude criticism and make us forget that there is any other Music of the same kind existing."[5] Indeed, Corelli had not simply "cleared the ground" for his own music; it seems he had also paved the way for other Italian violinist-composers, many of whom streamed across the English channel on the coattails of their illustrious Roman countryman to take advantage of a growing economy and a relatively free economic system that provided more opportunities to earn fame and fortune than any other place in Europe. Johann Mattheson noted this situation in 1713 when he wrote that "whoever wishes to achieve something in music these days makes for England. Italy and France are good for listening and learning; England is good for earning; Germany is good only for eating and drinking."[6] Samuel Sharp made the same observation fifty years later, in 1765, writing that an Italian performer, "if he be well advised, will certainly set out for *England,* where talents of every kind are rewarded ten-fold what they are at *Naples.*"[7]

Some of the Italian musicians who appeared in the British Isles during this period only made brief visits, as did Francesco Veracini (1690–1768) in 1714 and 1733. Others chose to stay, such as Felice Giardini (1716–96), Francesco Barsanti (1690–1772), and two pupils of Corelli: Pietro Castrucci (1679–1752) and Francesco Geminiani (1687–1762). Burney called Giardini "the greatest performer in Europe."[8] Barsanti became one of the most sought-after oboe players in London.[9] Castrucci moved to London in 1715 and served as leader of Handel's opera orchestra for twenty-two years. Geminiani arrived a year earlier, in 1714, and went on to play a larger musical role in his adopted country than any of his Italian compatriots, serving as the teacher of Avison and many other important English musicians and patrons.

The list of Italian émigrés who settled in the major cities of the United Kingdom is indeed long and distinguished.[10] Among them was a member of one of the most renowned musical families of Italy and the composer of the music of this edition: Francesco Scarlatti.

Francesco (Antonio Nicola) Scarlatti

Although the younger brother of the illustrious oratorio and opera composer Alessandro Scarlatti (1660–1725), and therefore the uncle of the great harpsichord composer Domenico Scarlatti (1685–1757), Francesco Scarlatti left few traces of his musical activity and family legacy.[11] Born in Palermo on 5 December 1666, Francesco moved to Naples at some point between 1672 and 1674 to further his musical studies. He was appointed as second violin in the royal court on 17 February 1684—the day that Alessandro was hired to replace retiring maestro di cappella Pietro Andrea Ziani (1616–84).[12]

The arrival of the Sicilian Scarlattis was not an entirely welcome event at the Neapolitan court, at least at the outset. One person who did not receive the Scarlatti family with open arms was Francesco Provenzale (1624–1704), a native Neapolitan and a respected opera composer at the theater at San Bartolomeo who had served as honorary head of the royal chapel since 1680. Provenzale fully expected to succeed Ziani as maestro di cappella, and he was so enraged by Alessandro's appointment that he resigned and took six singers with him.[13]

The Scarlatti clan also seems to have used some highly questionable methods to secure and consolidate their power in Naples. Nepotism was one such tactic, as we have seen in Alessandro's maneuver to hire Francesco on the same day he became maestro di cappella. The Scarlattis were also accused of selling positions to the highest bidders and of engaging in a variety of political intrigues. Matters were made far worse by their sister Anna Maria Scarlatti, who was also in residence in Naples during this time—ostensibly to establish or further her career as an opera singer.[14] In Naples, the "city of pleasures," it was not uncommon for officials at the court to keep opera singers as mistresses, and Anna Maria seems to have taken full advantage of these opportunities.[15] According to the Neapolitan diarist Domenico Confuroto, Anna Maria owed her success to her sexual relationships with various members of the court. His description of the reputation of the Scarlattis at the time is vivid and unflinching:

> At the beginning of November [1684] the Secretary of Justice, named Don Giovanni de Leone, Don Emmanuel ***, majordomo, who was also Governor of Pozzuoli, and a favorite page were stripped of their offices and disgraced by the signor Viceroy, because they maintained close and illicit relations with certain actresses, one of whom was called la Scarlati [sic], whose brother was made *maestro di capella* of the Palace by the said Viceroy in competition with other patriotic virtuosi. Because they set up a triumvirate, disposing at their will of the appointments and offices customarily awarded, giving them to those who offered and paid them the highest price and committing other illegal acts to make money and to please their whore-actresses; and they did that without the knowledge of the signor Viceroy, who, when he had been advised of everything, deprived them of their offices, as I said, and disgraced them; and he ordered the Scarlati and her female companions either to leave this city or to shut themselves up in a convent, and in conformity with this order, they placed themselves in the monastery of Santo Antoniello near the Vicaria.[16]

Despite such an inauspicious beginning for the Scarlatti family (or at least for its reputation), Francesco was able to enjoy a relatively successful career as a violinist in Naples for a number of years.[17] In 1690 he married Rosolina Albano, with whom he had five children.[18] He left Naples for Sicily in February 1691, however, and earned a living as a violinist in Palermo for the next twenty-four years.[19]

On 29 June 1715 Scarlatti applied for the position of vice-kapellmeister to Emperor Charles VI at the Viennese court and appeared in Vienna in person that year to audition for the job. He won the approval of the kapellmeister J. J. Fux, who reported to the emperor that he found Scarlatti "very suitable for this service, because of his expertise and rather high qualities."[20] Despite exaggerating his credentials and asserting his loyalty to the Austrian throne, however, Scarlatti did not win the position.[21]

Francesco had returned to Italy by 1719 (and probably earlier), but he moved to London during that year to join the large group of Italian expatriates who had made the British Isles their home.[22] Scarlatti's name can be found in a number of concert announcements in London between 1719 and 1724, including performances at the Hickford Room on 1 May 1719, 1 September 1720, and 16 March 1724. The advertisement for the concert on 1 September tells us that the program featured "the greatest part of [Francesco's] own composition," and it reminded readers that he was the "brother to the famous Allessandro [sic]."[23]

We lose track of Francesco's activities until 1733, when we learn that he had established residence in Dublin.[24] It is possible that he made the move to Dublin on the recommendation of two English Italophiles, Thomas Roseingrave and Matthew Dubourg, or perhaps that of Geminiani himself.[25] The news of Francesco was not promising, however; his marriage to a woman named Jane had ended—and, it seems, not amicably. The following notice appeared in *Faulkner's Dublin Journal* of 11–14 August 1733: "Whereas JANE SCARLATTI, wife of FRANCIS SCARLATTI, Master of Musick had eloped from her said Husband. This is to desire that no Body may give any Credit to the said Jane Scarlatti on account of her said Husband; for he will not pay any Debts that she shall contract; nor answer any Bills she may draw on him. April 7th 1733. Francis Scarlatti."[26]

The next and final traces of Francesco Scarlatti are found in 1741. A notice in the *Dublin Newletter* reported that a benefit concert had been organized for him on Friday, 13 February, and that Scarlatti was obviously seriously ill at this point. It is somewhat fitting that the concert was held in a hall owned by another Italian émigré, the "Musick Room" Geminiani had opened in Dublin in 1740.[27] The announcement of the concert, which had originally been scheduled for 7 February but later moved to the thirteenth, appeared in the *Dublin Newsletter* of 27–31 January 1741: "For the Benefit of Signior SCARLATI [sic], who has been confin'd near four months thro' Sickness. At Geminiani's Musick Room in Damestreet, on Saturday the 7th of February, will be performed a CONCERT OF MUSICK. In which Mr Dubourg will perform a solo, and Mr Worsdale sing some Songs. Three Ticket[s] Half a Guinea; single Tickets a British Crown."[28] There is no further information about Francesco Scarlatti after this date, and it is assumed that he died at some point in 1741. No grave has yet been found.

The Music of the Edition

Francesco Scarlatti left behind few compositions. The majority of his surviving music is for voice and includes cantatas, oratorios, and other sacred works, which he wrote during his residency in Italy.[29] Prior to the discovery of the concerti grossi of this edition, there was only one known instrumental work, a Sinfonia in C Major.

These concertos therefore not only represent a significant addition to the total known output of Francesco Scarlatti, but they also enhance our appreciation and understanding of the musical activities of the entire Scarlatti family. In addition, Scarlatti's concertos contribute to a more complete picture of the importance and development of the concerto grosso during the eighteenth century, particularly in England.

Although it is not possible to determine with certainty when the concertos were composed, it is likely that Scarlatti wrote them in London in an effort to win the favor of British audiences and satisfy their insatiable demand for works of this genre. Whether Scarlatti achieved this goal is difficult to ascertain, since no reviews or contemporary accounts exist to describe the reception of these compositions. Nevertheless, Scarlatti's concertos are fine examples of the genre. The writing for strings is idiomatic and fluent, and several passages call for a degree of virtuosity among the players. As one might expect, many such virtuosic moments occur in the solo sections for the first violin (e.g., Concerto No. 8 in F Major, II, mm. 46–56 and Concerto No. 9 in D Major, I, mm. 13–18); more novel are soloistic passages for the viola (e.g., Concerto No. 9, II, mm. 51–52). Scarlatti's approach to instrumental sonorities is often quite distinctive (e.g., the passage in parallel octaves between viola and bass in the Concerto No. 1 in E Major, I, m. 14). The same can be said about his harmonic language, such as in his use of suspensions over a pedal (Concerto No. 9, II, mm. 55–59 and Concerto No. 8, II, mm. 66–70).

Scarlatti employs a mixture of the *da chiesa* and *da camera* styles throughout these concertos. For example, the entire Concerto No. 4 in E Minor adheres to the standard *da chiesa* four-movement, slow-fast-slow-fast sequence, and the multisection first movement of Concerto No. 9 is also typical of the *da chiesa* style. Several concertos include dance movements common to the *da camera* style, though Scarlatti never labeled them as such. Concerto No. 1 includes both a sarabande in the third movement and a minuet in the fourth. Other sarabandes appear in the third movement of the Concerto No. 3 in A Minor and the second and third movements of Concerto No. 8. The final movements of the eighth and ninth concertos are written in gigue style, the former of which is in binary form.

Notes on Performance

When performing concerti grossi of the seventeenth and eighteenth centuries, a number of issues of historical performance practice need to be addressed, including size of ensemble, proportions of instruments in the *concertino* and *ripieno* groups, and use of embellishment. Since Francesco Scarlatti's concertos were most likely composed and performed for an English audience, a British source from the period would be the most reliable guide. Fortunately, such a guide exists in the writings of Charles Avison. Avison wrote more extensively about what he considered the proper performance of his concerti grossi than did almost any other composer of the baroque era. Moreover, Avison's recently discovered workbooks provide the only source of the Scarlatti concerti grossi of this edition (see the critical report). Avison's writings on performance practice, which we find in the prefaces to his published works and in his polemical treatise *An Essay on Musical Expression* (1752), are specific, detailed, and presented in a clear and unambiguous style. By following Avison's instructions, performers today can arrive at an interpretation that would have been recognizable to Avison and other composers active in England during the eighteenth century. The remainder of this section draws from the preface to Avison's Six Concertos in Seven Parts, op. 3 (1751).

Addressing matters of ensemble size, Avison wrote that the ideal balance of instruments in the orchestra is a *concertino* group consisting of four players—solo first and second violins, solo viola, and solo cello (it is to be assumed that a harpsichord was also part of this group)—and a large *ripieno* ensemble of six first violins and four second violins, four cellos, and two double basses. Always a practical musician, Avison nonetheless remained flexible about the number of players for the *ripieno*, as long as the overall balance was maintained: "A lesser Number of Instruments, near the same Proportion, will also have a proper Effect, and may answer the Composer's Intention; but more would probably destroy the just Contrast, which should always be kept up between the *Chorus* and *Solo*." Avison cautioned against doubling any of the *concertino* instruments, since this "wou'd be an Impropriety in the Conduct of our Musical Oeconomy," and he defended his use of the seemingly large number of cellos in the *ripieno*, despite the fact that some critics would think that they "wou'd be found too powerful for the *Violins*." He also insisted that a double bass always be used, "especially in a Performance of full Concertos, as they cannot be heard to any Advantage without that Noble Foundation of their Harmony."

Avison often addressed issues of performance practice with a sharp tongue likely honed from years of dealing with the amateur musicians who filled the tutti sections of orchestras of the period. For example, he felt compelled to ask for something that should be self-evident: before performing a concerto, a player should study his part and the score, and practice. "For Instance, how often does the Fate of a Concerto depend in the temerarious Execution of a Sett of Performers, who have never previously considered the Work, examined the Connection of its Parts, or studied the Intention of the Whole?" Performance and rehearsal levels must have been frustratingly low indeed in England at this time, since Avison complained that his players, including the soloists, were unable to maintain a steady rhythm: "In the four principal Parts, there ought to be four Performers of almost equal Mastery; as well in regard to *Time,* as Execution; for however easy it may seem to acquire the former, yet nothing more shews a Master than a steady Performance throughout the whole Movement."

Avison also criticized players for their inability to realize the dynamics exactly as they were written, finding it necessary to remind performers to keep "strict Regard . . . to the *Piano* and *Forte*" since they often "pass unobserved, or at all express'd, in so careless and negligent a manner as to produce little, if any, sensible difference to the Hearer." It also appears that the temptation to create a diminuendo by reducing the number of instruments, rather than by simply playing softer, was as strong in the eighteenth century as it is today. Avison condemned "those lukewarm Performers, who imagine that diminishing the number of Instruments will answer the same End as softening the whole, to quit their Part when they shou'd rather be all Attention how to manage it with the utmost Delicacy." Elsewhere Avison warned "unexperienced performers" against making the very common mistake of slowing down in a diminuendo or speeding up for a crescendo.[30]

Turning to the important question of embellishment, particularly by members of the *ripieno* section, Avison's answer is unequivocal: tutti players are allowed no ornamentation or octave transpositions. "In every Part throughout the full Chorus, all manner of Graces or diminution of Passages, or Transposition of eight Notes higher, must be avoided; which some indiscrete Performers are but too apt to make use of . . . but these Gentlemen ought to consider, that by such Liberties they do not only disappoint the expecting Ear . . . but often introduce and occasion *Disallowances* in the Harmony."

An accomplished keyboard player, Avison not surprisingly devoted a considerable amount of time and space to the proper performance on the harpsichord in concerti grossi and other ensemble pieces. His instructions, at least to players of modest abilities, are simple and specific: play the correct chords, keep a steady rhythm, do not fill in rests with extraneous embellishments or passage work, and do not add connecting material to the first endings of repeated sections. Avison also advised these harpsichordists to use with discretion *acciaccaturas* and other techniques typical of harpsichord arpeggiation:

> As [the harpsichord] is only to be used in the Chorus, the Performer will have little else to regard but the striking just Chords, keeping the Time and being careful, that no jangling Sound, or scattering of the Notes be continued after the *Pause* or *Cadence* . . . the same Care is necessary at the return of each *double Strain*, when there are no intermediate Notes to introduce the *Repeat*. In fine, a profound Silence must always be observed, wherever the Composer has intended a general Respit, or Pause in the Work. I am the more particular in giving this Caution to Performers on the Harpsichord, as they are the most liable to transgress in this way; because their Instrument, lying so commodious to their Fingers, is ever tempting them to run, like Wild-fire, over the Keys, and thus perpetually interrupt the Performance. . . . The Use of *Acciaccatura* or sweeping of the Chords, and the *dropping* or *sprinkling* Notes, are indeed some of the peculiar Beauties of this Instrument. But these graceful *Touches* are only reserved for a Masterly Application on the Accompanyment of a fine Voice or single Instrument.

When grappling with questions of historical performance in baroque concerti grossi, modern musicians should not find it difficult to follow Avison's instructions. So clearly expressed, Avison's writings make much practical sense when applied to his music and that of his contemporaries—including the concerti grossi of Francesco Scarlatti.

Notes

1. The continued loyalty of Charles II to France was understandable, particularly because Louis XIV provided Charles with financial support to enable him to remain independent of Parliament.

2. They also returned with actual "souvenirs" from Italy, including paintings, drawings, and printed music. Roger North, for example, tells us that "the numerous traine of yong travelers of the best quality and estates . . . about this time went over into Italy and resided at Rome and Venice, where they heard the best musick and learnt of the best masters . . . [and] came home confirmed in the love of the Italian manner." John Wilson, ed., *Roger North on Music* (London: Novello, 1959), 310. One beneficiary of the English tradition of the Grand Tour was Colonel John Blaithwaite, who served as a director of the Royal Academy for Music. Blaithwaite had not only visited Italy but also studied with none other than Alessandro Scarlatti as a child. Hawkins tells us that "this gentleman, an officer in the army, had when a child been a pupil of Alessandro Scarlatti: His proficiency on the harpsichord at twelve years of age astonished everyone." John Hawkins, *A General History of the Science and Practice of Music*, 2 vols. (London, 1853), 2:860n, quoted in George E. Dorris, *Paolo Rolli and the Italian Circle in London, 1715–1744* (The Hague: Mouton, 1967), 78 n. 83.

3. Wilson, *Roger North on Music*, 307, quoted in Enrico Careri, *Francesco Geminiani (1687–1762)* (Oxford: Clarendon, 1993), 8 n. 3.

4. For further information on Avison and his role in the development of the concerto grosso in England, see the critical report and my edition of Charles Avison, *Concerto Grosso Arrangements of Geminiani's Opus 1 Violin Sonatas*, Recent Researches in the Music of the Baroque Era, vol. 160 (Middleton, Wis.: A-R Editions, 2010).

5. Charles Burney, *A General History of Music from the Earliest Ages to the Present Period*, ed. Frank Mercer, 2 vols. (London, 1935; repr., New York: Dover, 1957), 2:442.

6. Johann Mattheson, *Das neu-eröffnete Orchestre* (Hamburg: Schiller, 1713), 211, quoted in Careri, *Francesco Geminiani*, 9.

7. Samuel Surgeon Sharp, *Letters from Italy, Describing the Customs and Manners of that Country, in the Years 1765, and 1766* (London: R. Cave, 1766), 80.

8. Burney, *General History of Music*, 2:895.

9. According to Hawkins, Barsanti arrived with Geminiani in London in 1714. Hawkins, *General History*, 2:896. David Lasocki, however, believes that Barsanti arrived some years later, probably in 1723, noting that Barsanti "does not appear in the list of six oboe players examined in 1720 for four posts in the

xii

opera orchestra of the Royal Academy of Music." See David Lasocki, "Professional Recorder Players in England 1540–1740" (Ph.D. diss., University of Iowa, 1983), 846, quoted in Careri, *Francesco Geminiani*, 8 n. 2.

10. For a comprehensive discussion of the numerous Italian musicians wandering the British Isles during this period, see Simon McVeigh, "Italian Violinists in Eighteenth Century London," in *The Eighteenth-Century Diaspora of Italian Music and Musicians*, ed. Reinhard Strom (Brepols: Turnhout, 2001), 139–76.

11. There is no biography of Francesco Scarlatti, but information about his life and career can be found in a number of sources, including Brian Boydell, *A Dublin Musical Calendar 1700–1760* (Blackrock: Irish Academic Press, 1988); Careri, *Francesco Geminiani*; Edward J. Dent, *Alessandro Scarlatti: His Life and Works* (1905; repr. with preface and additional notes by Frank Walker, London: Edward Arnold, 1960); Donald Jay Grout, *Alessandro Scarlatti* (Berkeley: University of California Press, 1979); Ulisse Proto Giurleo, *Alessandro Scarlatti, "il Palermitano" (la patria & la famiglia)* (Naples: Lubrano, 1926); and Roberto Pagano, *Alessandro and Domenico Scarlatti: Two Lives in One*, trans. Frederick Hammond (New York: Pendragon, 2006).

12. Francesco arrived from Palermo as a "small child, who was not marriageable, since he could not be more than six or seven years old." Proto Giurleo, *Alessandro Scarlatti*, 21, quoted in Pagano, *Alessandro and Domenico Scarlatti*, 22.

13. The sixty-year-old Provenzale probably realized that he had little chance of removing Alessandro or waiting for him to leave, since Alessandro was only thirty-four years old when he became maestro di cappella. See Dinko Fabris, *Music in Seventeenth-Century Naples* (Aldershot: Ashgate, 2007), 224; and Grout, *Alessandro Scarlatti*, 51.

14. Although there is little documentation about the operatic roles performed by Italian singers of this period, Anna Maria Scarlatti's opera career was probably quite limited. There is no record of her singing in Rome, and the only role she sang in Venice was a small part in Pietro Simone Agostini's *Il ratto delle Sabine* at the Teatro S. Giovanni Crisostomo in 1689. Dent, *Alessandro Scarlatti*, 36.

15. Ibid.

16. Domenico Confuroto, *Giornali di Napoli dal MDCLXXIX al MDCIC*, ed. Nicola Nicolini (Naples: Lubrano, 1930), 1:119, quoted in Pagano, *Alessandro and Domenico Scarlatti*, 22–23. Pagano raises the hypothesis that the source of this scandal was not Anna Maria, but rather another Scarlatti sister, Melchiorra Brigida, who was indeed an "actress." He ultimately concludes, however, that it was Anna Maria who engaged in "illegal" sexual activity. See Pagano, *Alessandro and Domenico Scarlatti*, 23.

17. Dent asserts that Francesco's stipend from the royal chapel was paid for only one year. Dent, *Alessandro Scarlatti*, 34. Pagano disagrees, citing Francesco's request in 1691 "for permission to betake himself to Palermo 'to attend to certain special interests of his.'" See Pagano, *Alessandro and Domenico Scarlatti*, 74.

18. His contract to marry Rosolina Albano was signed on 18 March 1690, and their first son Matteo was born on 23 December 1690. The other children were Antonio, Eleonora, Giovanni, and Dorotea. Rosolina died on 29 June 1706. Pagano, *Alessandro and Domenico Scarlatti*, 74.

19. It appears that Francesco was not a member of the royal chapel in Palermo, but rather a freelance musician, as can be seen by his membership in the city's Unione dei Musici in January and July 1694. *The New Grove Dictionary of Music and Musicians*, 2nd ed. (hereafter NG2), s.v. "Scarlatti, Francesco," by Christopher Hair. Pagano believes that Francesco's "special interests" in Palermo were to serve as a "semiclandestine surrogate for his brother, perhaps assigned to some church as a composer . . . and almost certainly employed to adapt scores by Alessandro to local necessities." See Pagano, *Alessandro and Domenico Scarlatti*, 74.

20. "Ich finde diesen Supplicanten wegen seiner virtù und sonst beywoneten gutten Aigenschafften sehr tauglich." L. von Köchel, *J. J. Fux, Hofcompositor und Hofkapellmeister* (Vienna, 1872), 378, quoted in Dent, *Alessandro Scarlatti*, 34. My translation.

21. Francesco claimed that he lost his position of maestro di cappella at Palermo after twenty-six years of service because he was a devoted sympathizer to Austria. Dent, however, tells us that "the archives in Palermo make no mention of him in this capacity, and Mongitore's diary expressly names Giuseppe Dia as Maestro di Capella in Palermo in 1703." Dent, *Alessandro Scarlatti*, 34–35. Pagano adds that Francesco told the court in Vienna that he "exercised the Post of Maestro di Capella in Palermo, with the universal indulgence of all the Virtuosi and Composers of Music," and that his service in Palermo lasted "for the course of 26 years." Fux obviously believed the job seeker, writing that Francesco had been driven from Palermo "by the enemies of the house of Austria." Pagano, *Alessandro and Domenico Scarlatti*, 75. See also Andrea Sommer-Mathis, "Entre Nápoles, Barcelona y Viena: Nuevos documentos sobre la circulación de músicos a principios del siglo XVIII," *Artigrama, Revista del Departemento de Historia del Arte de la Universidad de Zaragoza*, no. 12 (1996–97): *La circulación de música y músicos en la Europa mediterránea (ss. XVI–XVII)*: 45–77. Although Francesco did exaggerate his official position in Palermo and the number of years he served there, his sympathy for Austria was obviously genuine. Pagano tells us that a petition states that Francesco "was expelled ignominiously with his entire Family under punishment of death if he returned to that Country for the 'affection' shown by him for the Most August Imperial House," and that he left Naples for Barcelona before applying for the position in Vienna, although he was not successful in securing a position in Spain. See Pagano, *Alessandro and Domenico Scarlatti*, 75.

22. Hair suggests that he moved to London on the invitation of Geminiani or possibly even Handel, but no documentation exists to confirm this. NG2, "Scarlatti, Francesco."

23. Dent, *Alessandro Scarlatti*, 35; and Pagano, *Alessandro and Domenico Scarlatti*, 76. The announcements appeared in the *Daily Courant*.

24. The devotion to Italian music seems to have been as strong in Dublin as it was in London. Bernadette O'Neill offers the following contemporary description of this situation: "A stranger is agreeably surprised to find almost in every house he enters Italian airs saluting his ears. Corelli is a name in more mouths than many of their viceroys." Bernadette O'Neill, "Music in Dublin 1700–1780" (M.A. diss., University College, Dublin, 1971), 82, quoted in Careri, *Francesco Geminiani*, 32 n. 15.

25. Geminiani had established strong ties to Dublin during his long residence in the British Isles and was even offered a position in the city. When he declined, the post was given to his student Dubourg. Hawkins tells us that when John Sigismund Cousser, "the . . . master and composer of the state of music in Ireland . . . died in the year 1727," Geminiani's student and patron Lord Essex (William Capel, 1697–1743) offered his teacher a post in Dublin in 1728. Geminiani, however, "found that it was not tenable by one of the Romish communion, he therefore declined accepting it, assigning as a reason that he was a member of the catholic church. . . . Upon this refusal on the part of Geminiani, the place was bestowed on Mr. Matthew Dubourg, a young man who had been one of his pupils." John Hawkins, *A General History of the Science and Practice of Music*, 2 vols. (London, 1853; repr., New York: Dover, 1963), 2:847–8, quoted in Careri, *Francesco Geminiani*, 21. Nevertheless, Geminiani did visit Dublin in December 1733, arriving on the sixth and performing on the seventeenth. The *Dublin Evening Post* informed the public of Geminiani's arrival in their issues of 4–8 December 1733: "SIGNIOR GEMINIANI; a Native of Italy, and most famous Musician, arrived here with His Lordship." The newspaper announced Geminiani's concert in their issues of 11–15 December 1733: "GEMINIANI makes his Irish debut. Songs by Mrs Davis." Boydell, *Dublin Musical Calendar*, 55.

26. Ibid., 54.

27. According to the *Dublin Newsletter* of 26 April 1740, Geminiani also played a concert in the room during this visit to Dublin. The "Musick Room" remained open at least until 1782, when a show with "Chinese shadows" was presented there. Careri, *Francesco Geminiani*, 31–32.

28. Boydell, *Dublin Musical Calendar*, 70. The concert date of 7 February that appeared in the first two announcements was changed to 13 February in the subsequent two editions. According to Boydell, the notice also reported that "Signior Scarlotti, who, thro' a long Confinement by Sickness, is reduced to very distressful circumstances."

29. For example, a mass and a setting of Psalm 110 ("Dixit Dominus") are dated Palermo 1702 and 1703, respectively; *La profetessa guerriera* was performed in Palermo in 1703; and Francesco himself appeared in *Petracchio scremmetore* in Aversa in 1711. See Pagano, *Alessandro and Domenico Scarlatti*, 74 and 215.

30. In the preface to his Eight Concertos in Seven Parts, op. 4 (1760), Avison admonished those performers "with whom it is almost a general Practice to *abate* the *Time* where the Sounds are *diminished;* as also where the Sounds are *encreased* to *quicken* the *Time*." He concludes with the definitive statement that "we should neither *retard* the *Piano,* nor *precipitate* the *Forte*."

Plate 1. Francesco Scarlatti, Concerto No. 1 in E Major, first movement, measures 1–25. Newcastle City Library, Newcastle Collection, Charles Avison Archive, Workbook I, folio 2r. Reproduced with permission from the Avison Ensemble.

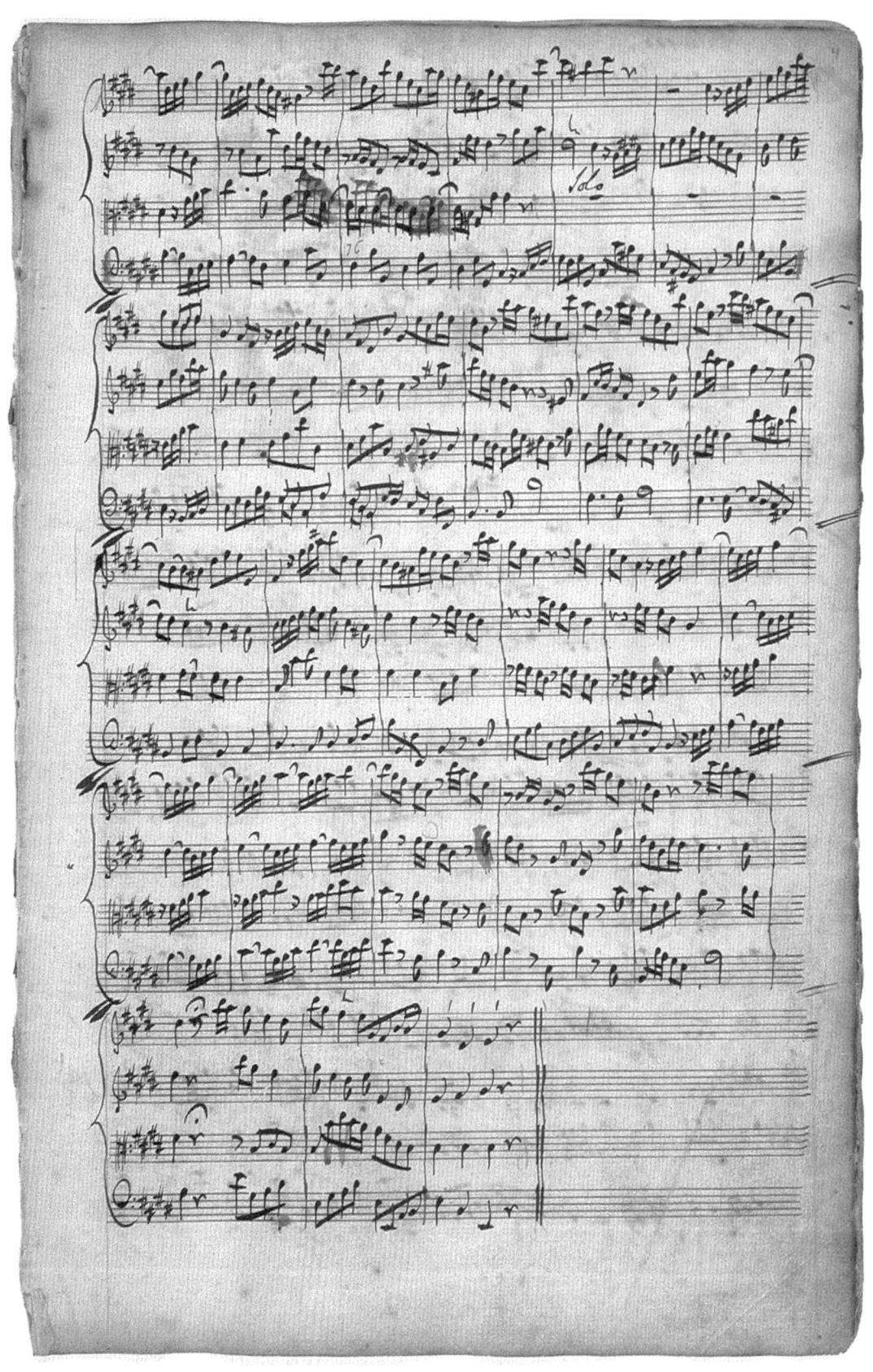

Plate 2. Francesco Scarlatti, Concerto No. 1 in E Major, third movement, measures 37–61. Newcastle City Library, Newcastle Collection, Charles Avison Archive, Workbook I, folio 4r. Reproduced with permission from the Avison Ensemble.

Plate 3. Francesco Scarlatti, Concerto No. 8 in F Major, second movement, measures 47–52. Newcastle City Library, Newcastle Collection, Charles Avison Archive, Workbook I, folio 18v. Reproduced with permission from the Avison Ensemble.

Plate 4. Francesco Scarlatti, Concerto No. 9 in D Major, fourth movement, measures 29–47. Newcastle City Library, Newcastle Collection, Charles Avison Archive, Workbook I, folio 22r. Reproduced with permission from the Avison Ensemble.

Concerto No. 1 in E Major

I

II

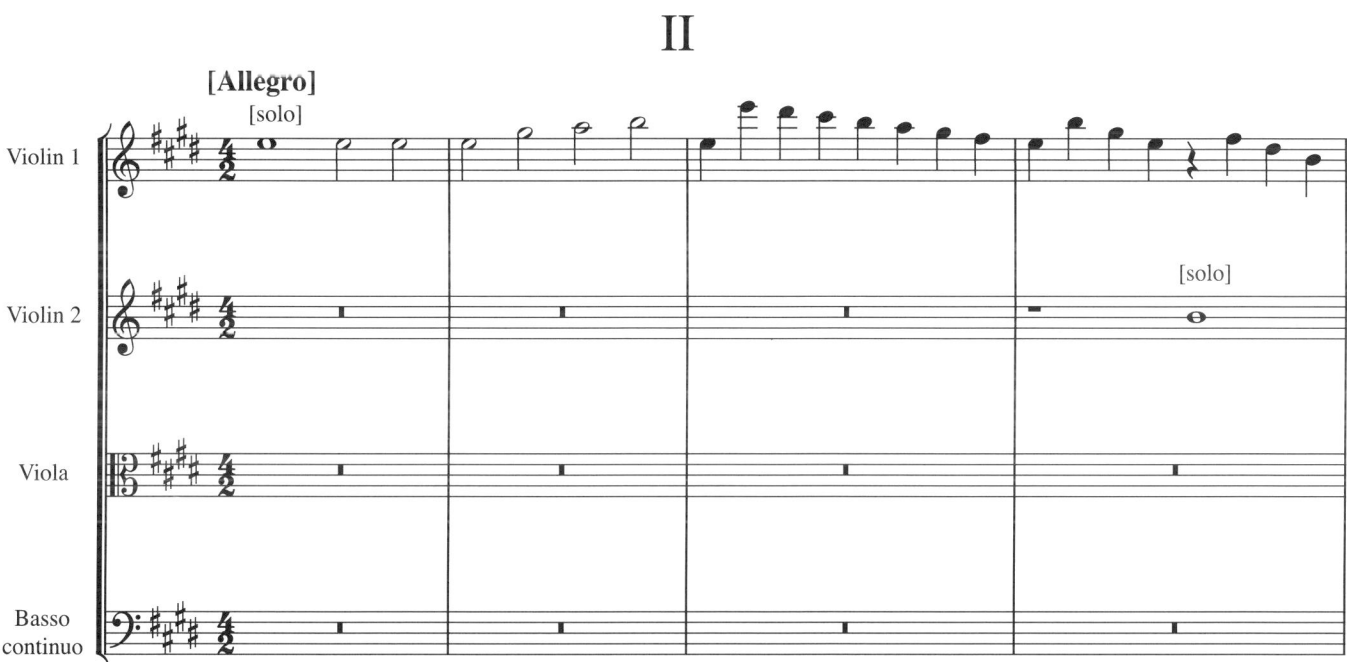

4

35
[tutti]
[tutti]
[tutti]
40
solo
tutti
solo
tutti
45

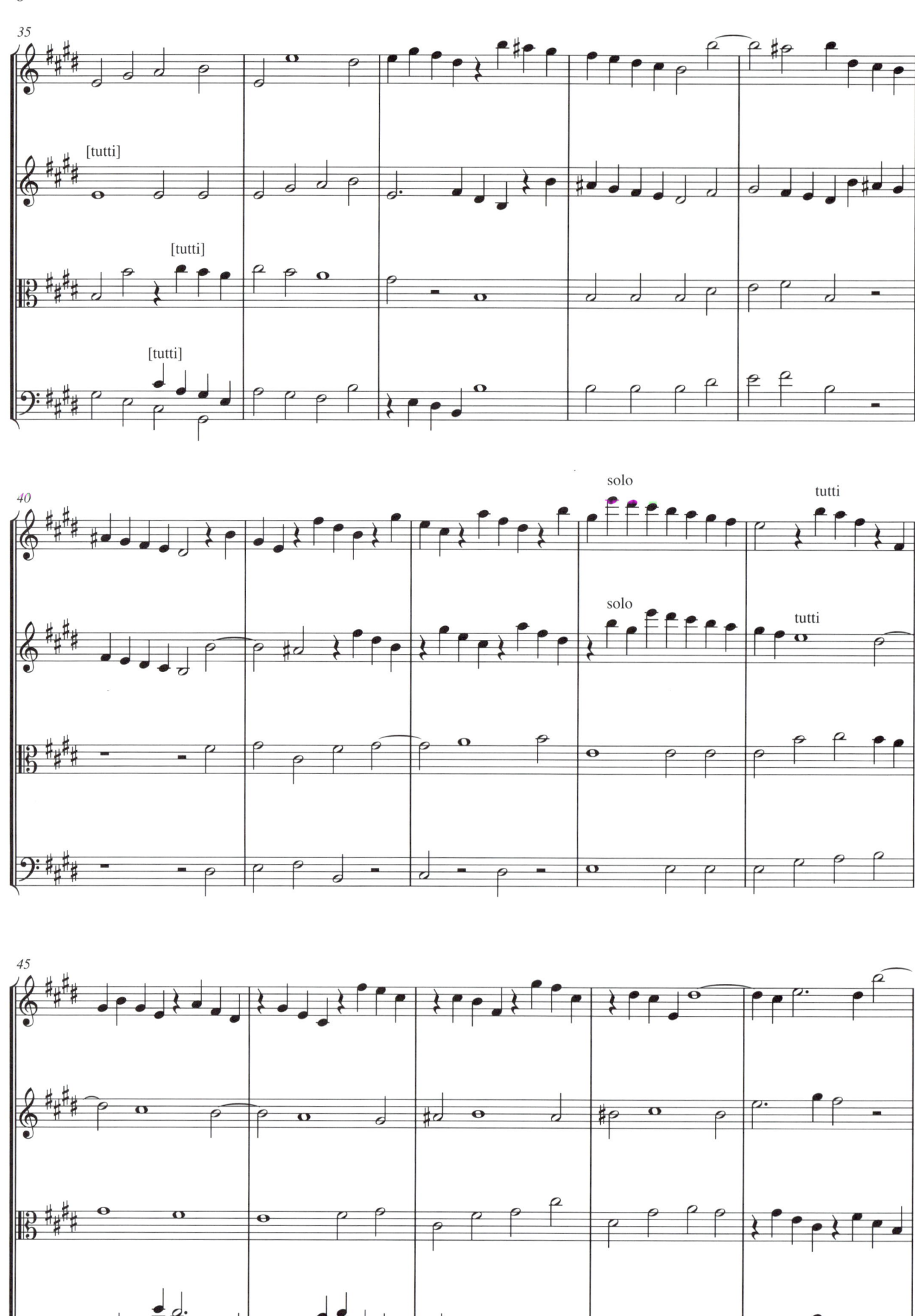

III

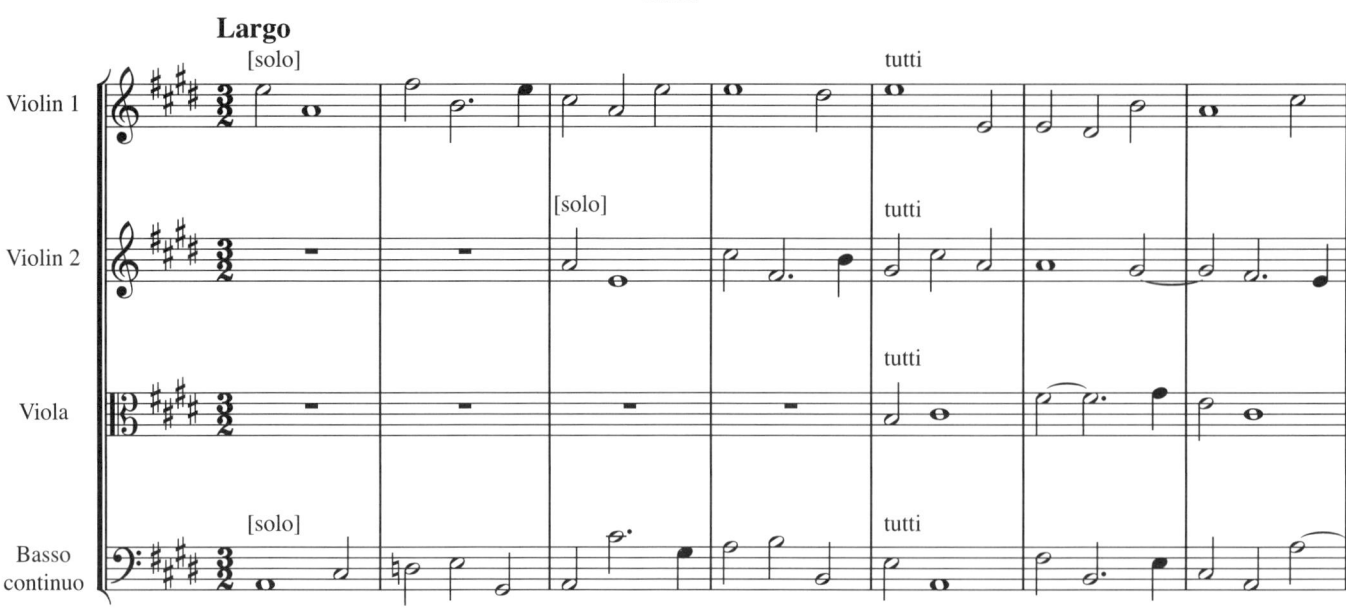

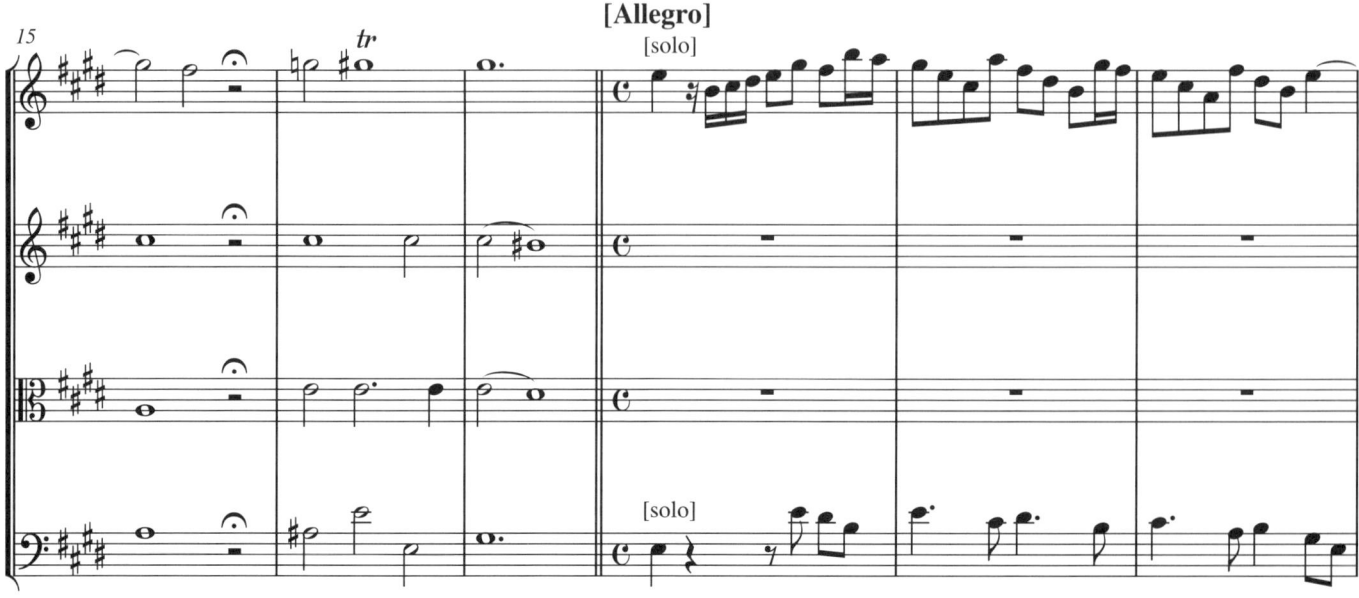

IV

20
tr
tr
p
p
p
p
27
tr
solo
tr
solo
[tr]
[tr]
tutti
tutti
solo
solo
solo
tutti
solo
34
tutti
tutti
solo
solo
tutti
solo

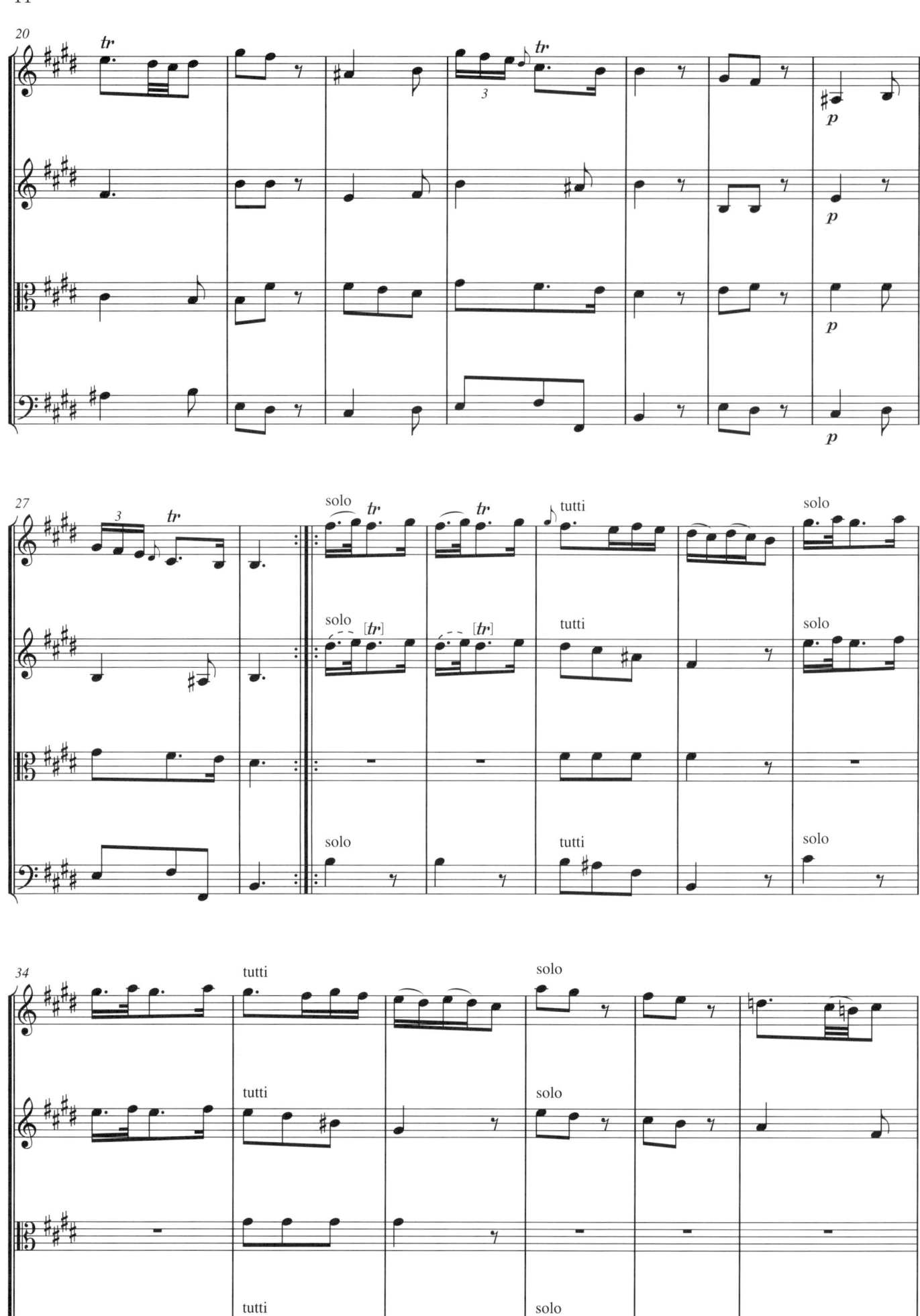

Concerto No. 2 in C Minor

I

II

19

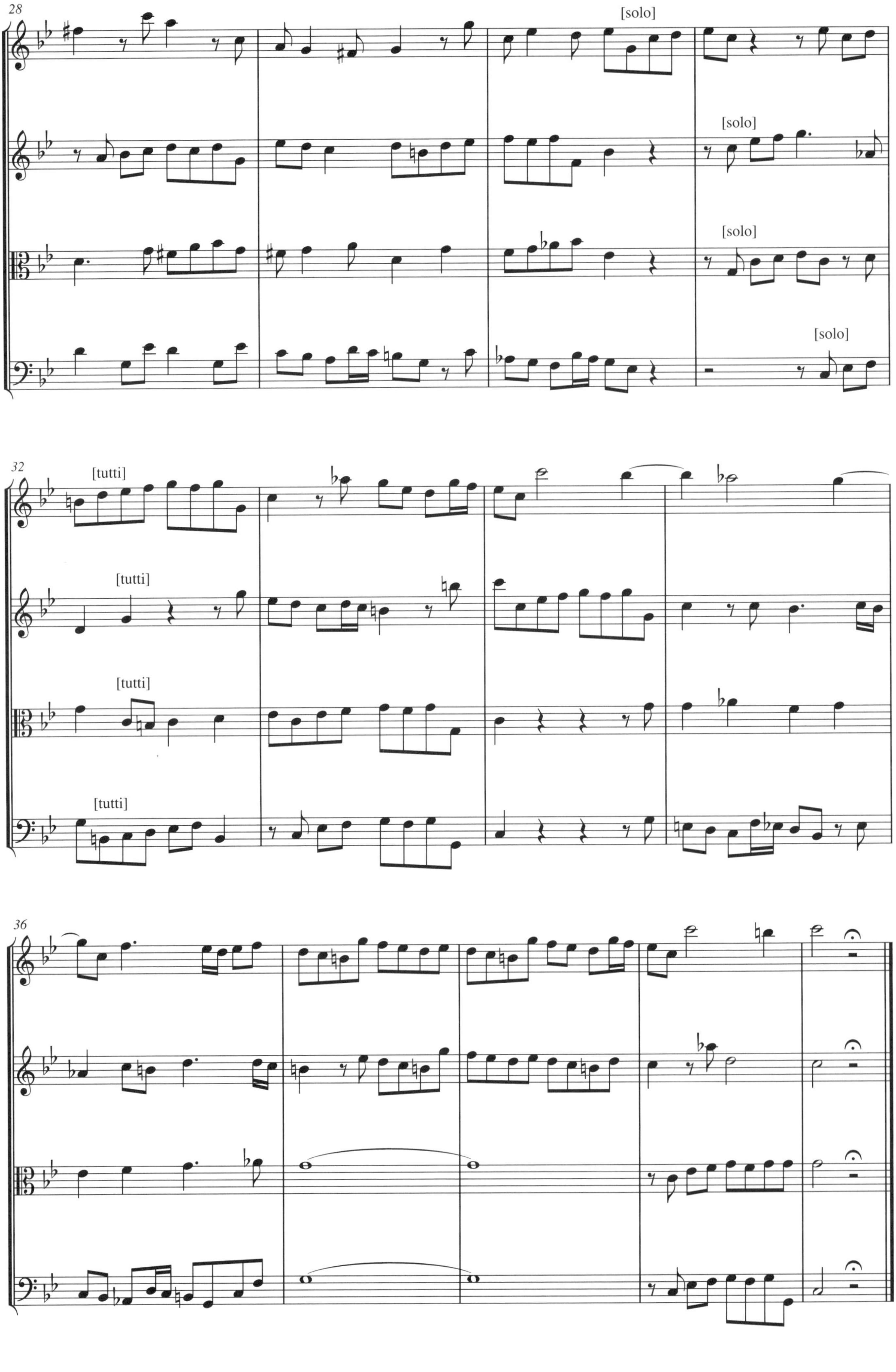
28
[solo]
[solo]
[solo]
[solo]
32
[tutti]
[tutti]
[tutti]
[tutti]
36

III
IV

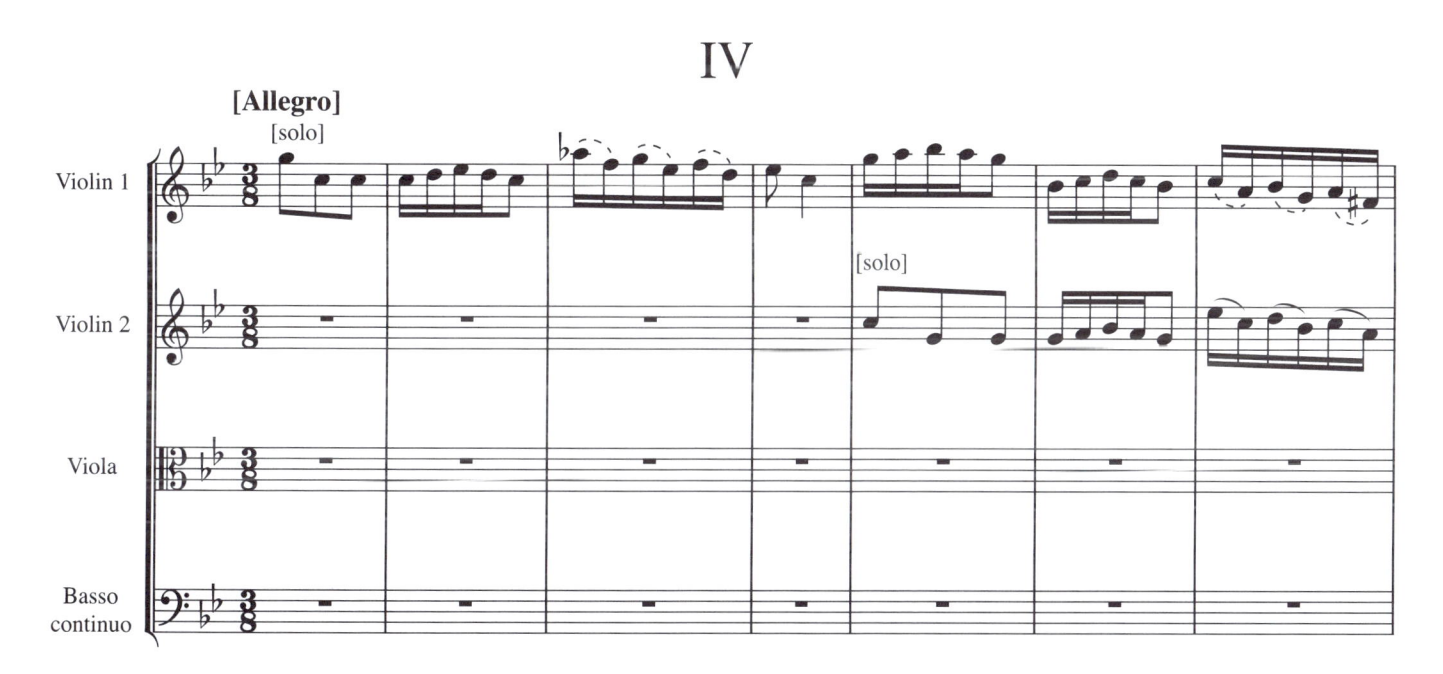

8
[solo]
[solo]
14
20
tutti
conc.
rip.
unis.
tutti
conc.
rip.
unis.
tutti
tutti

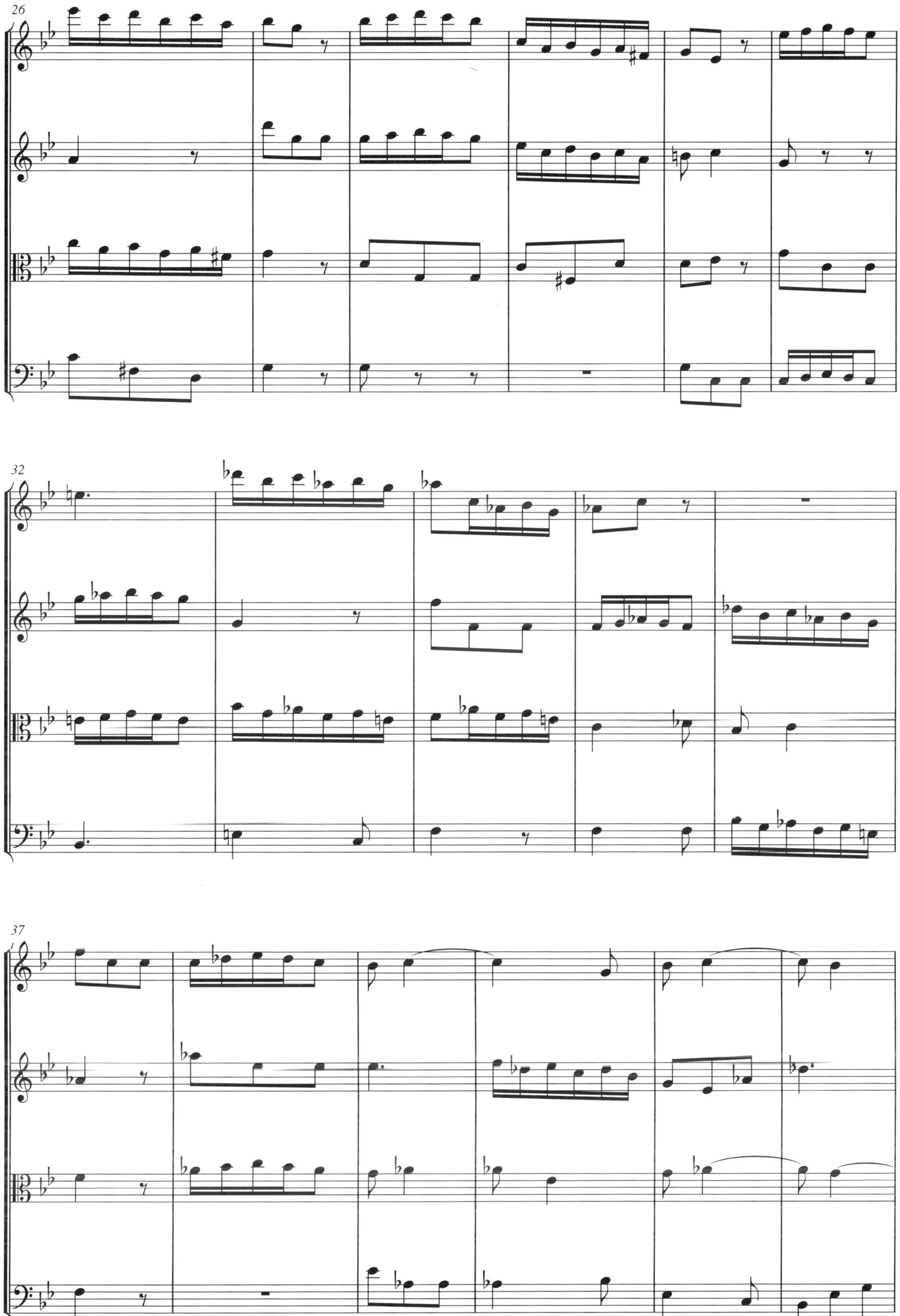
26
32
37

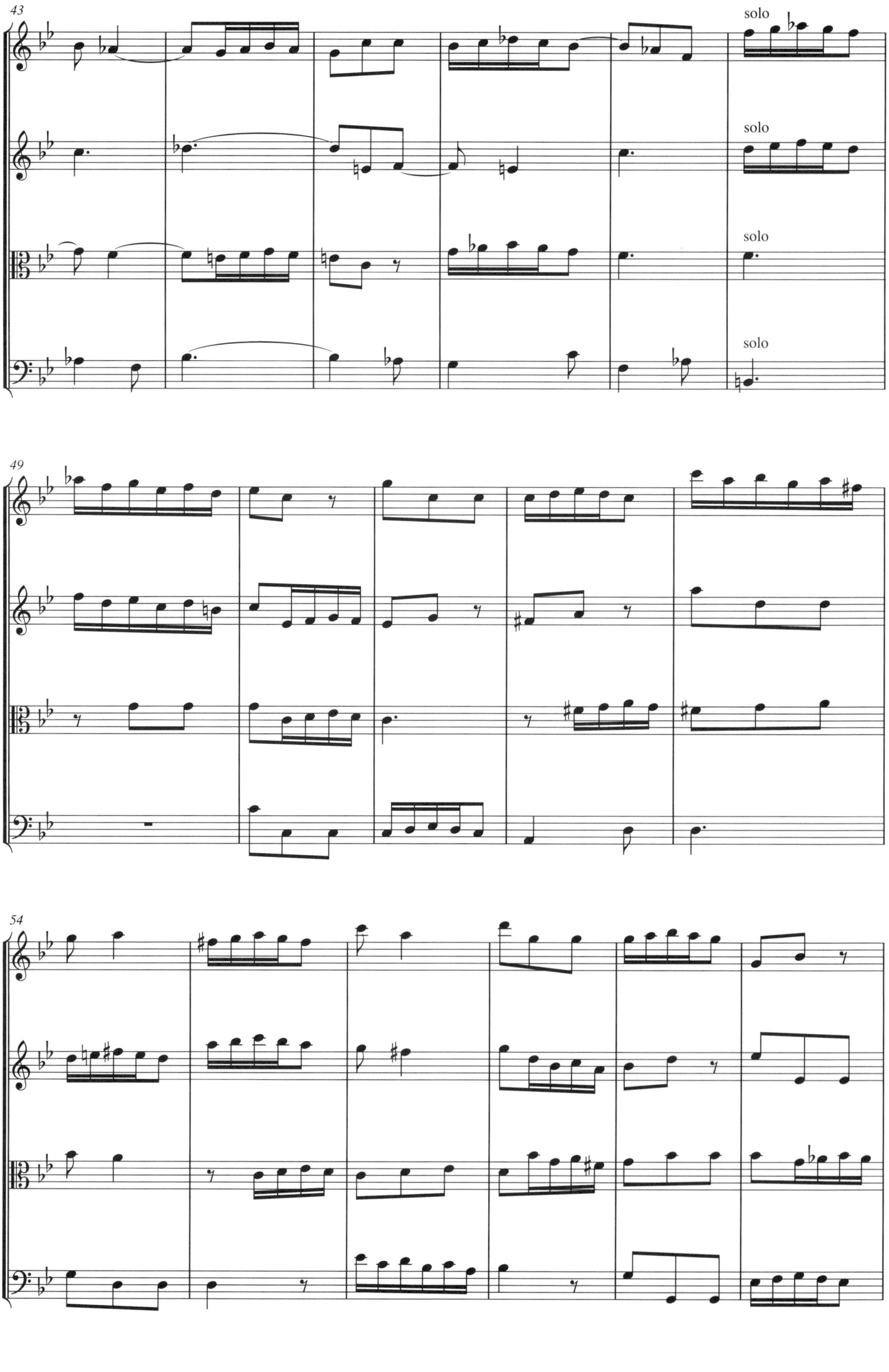
43
solo
solo
solo
solo
49
54

60
tutti
conc.
rip.
tutti
conc.
rip.
tutti
tutti
66
unis.
[solo]
unis.
[solo]
[solo]
[solo]
72
[tutti]
[tutti]
[tutti]
[tutti]

Concerto No. 3 in A Minor

I

II

12
[tutti]
[tutti]
[tutti]
[tutti]
16
[solo]
[solo]
[solo]
[solo]
tutti
tutti
tutti
tutti
20

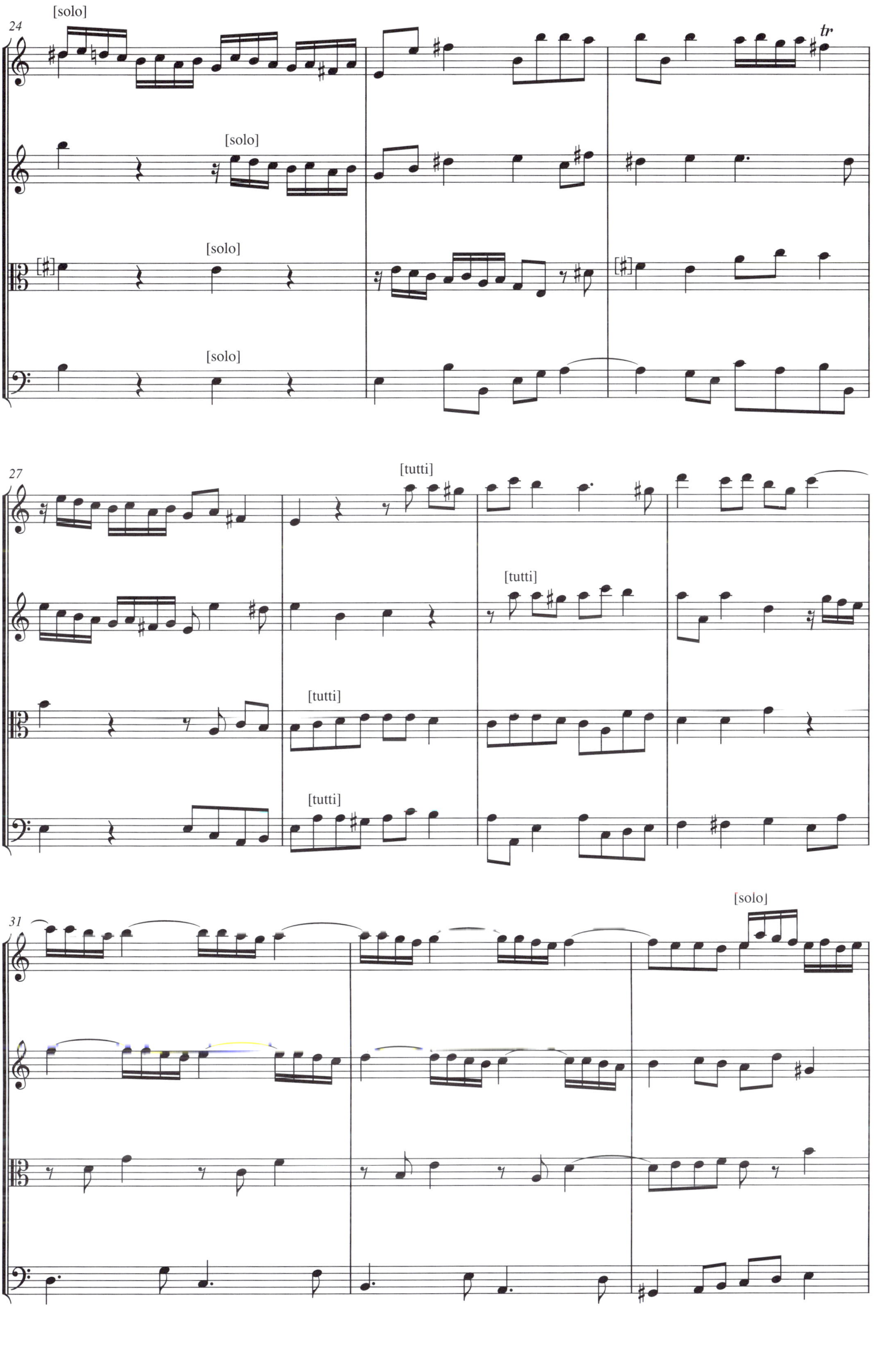
24
[solo]
tr
[solo]
[solo]
[solo]
27
[tutti]
[tutti]
[tutti]
[tutti]
31
[solo]

III

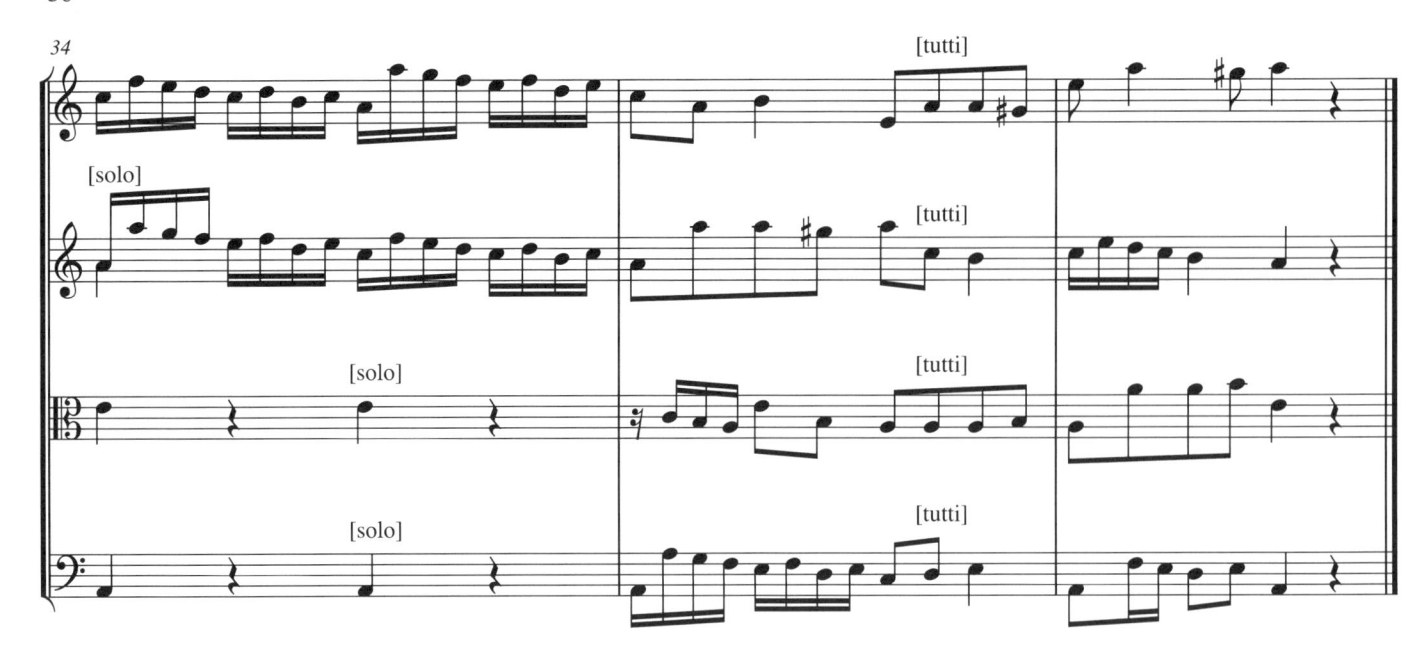

[Larghetto]

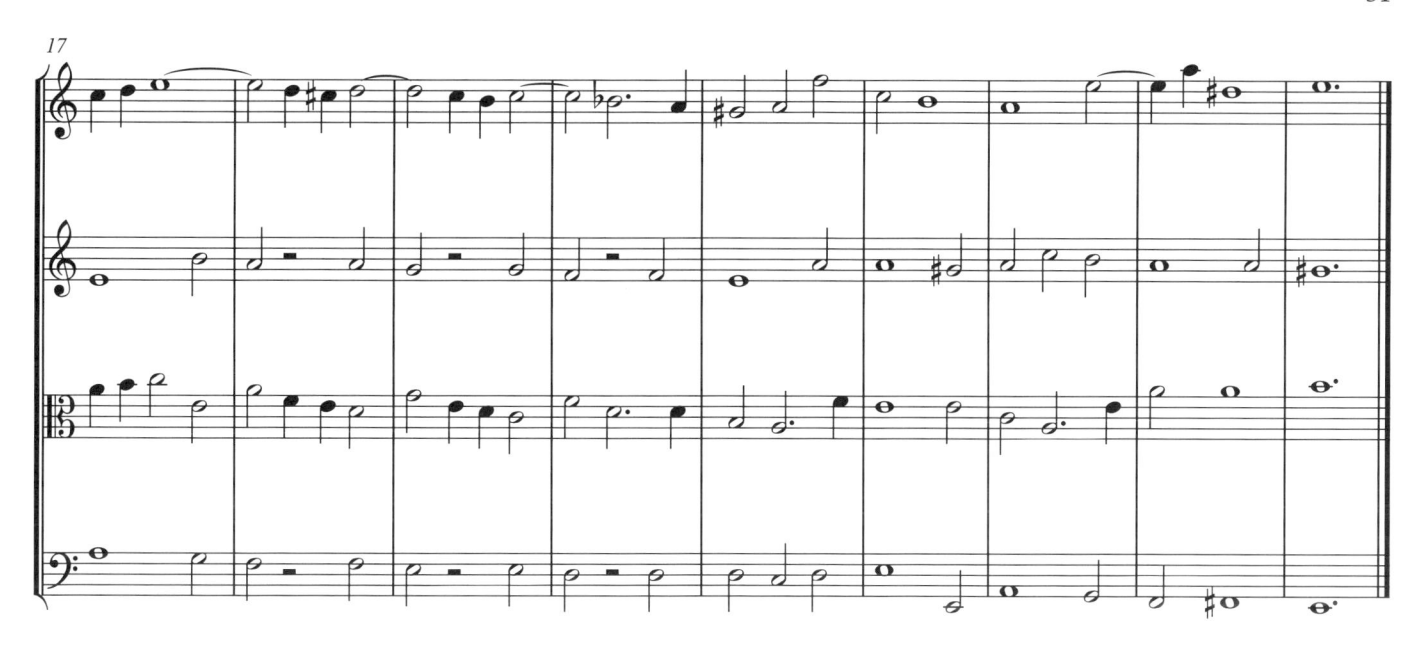

IV

[Allegro]

9
[tutti]
[tutti]
[tutti]
[tutti]
13
[solo]
[solo]
[solo]
[solo]
17
[tutti]
[tutti]
[tutti]
[tutti]

21
25
[solo]
[solo]
[solo]
[solo]
29
[tutti]
[solo]
[tutti]
[solo]
[tutti]
[solo]
[tutti]
[solo]

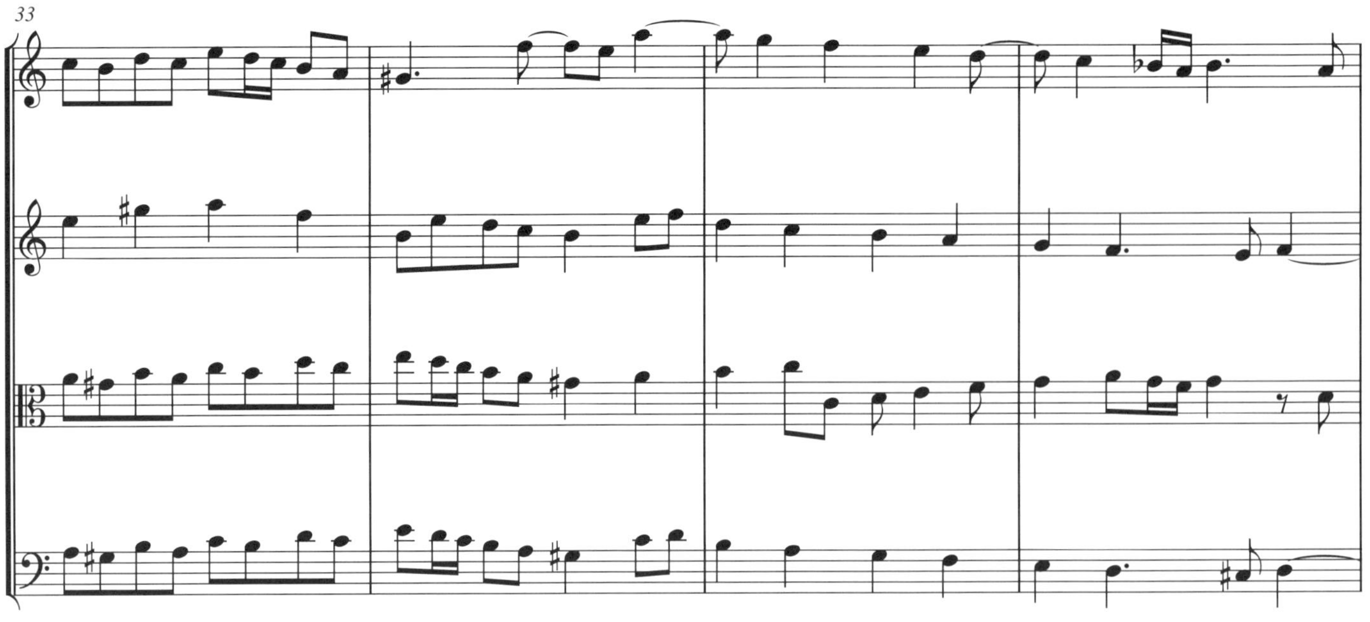
33

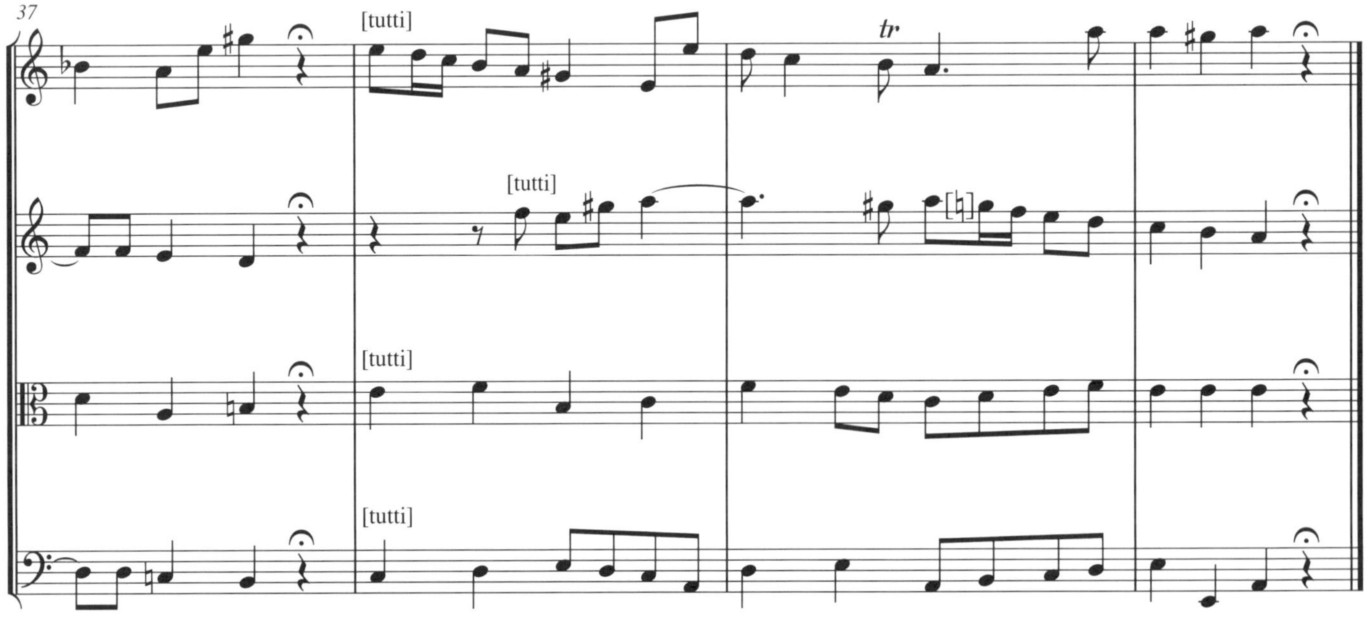
37
[tutti]
[tutti]
tr
[tutti]
[tutti]

Concerto No. 4 in E Minor

I

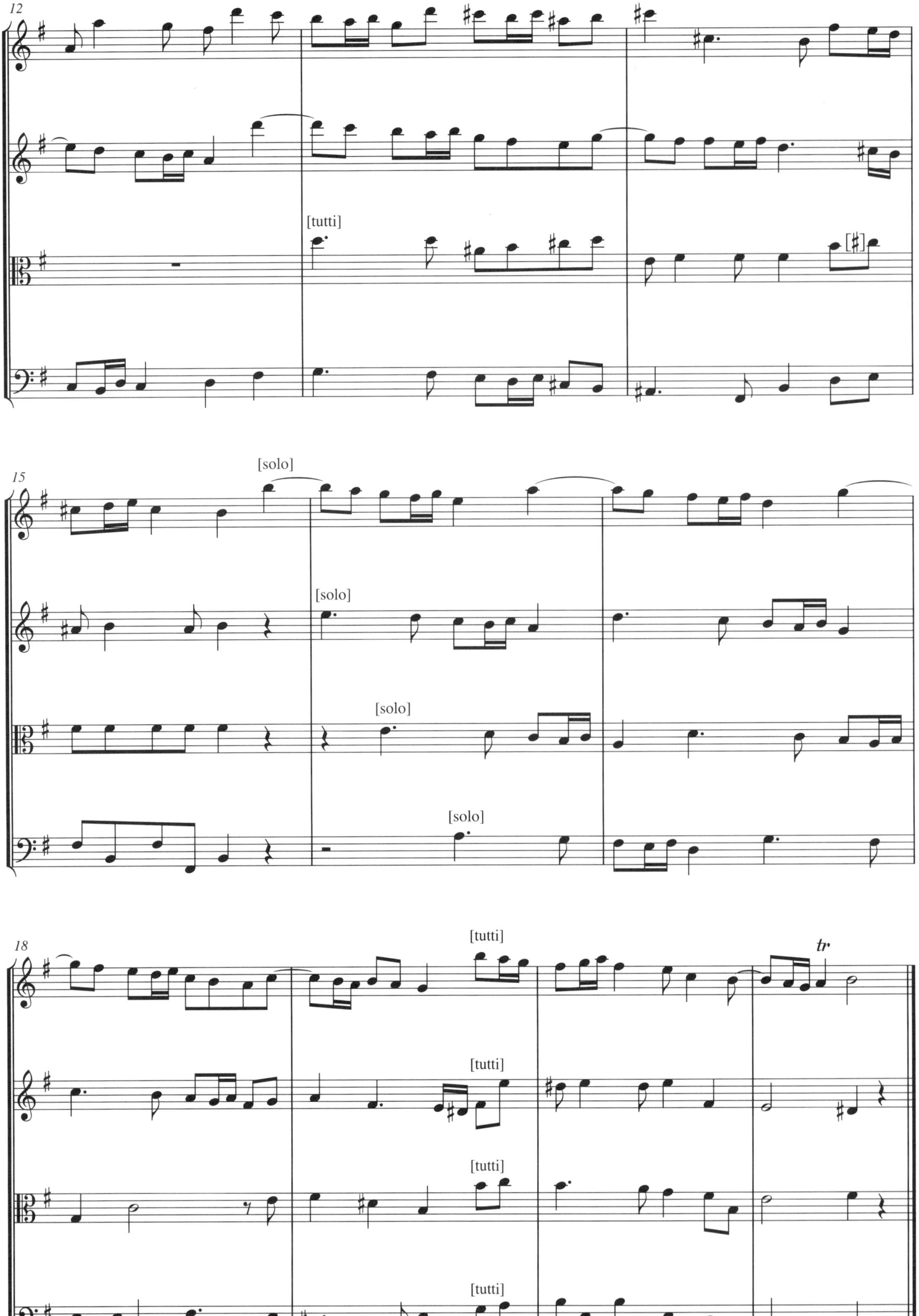
12
[tutti]
15
[solo]
[solo]
[solo]
[solo]
18
[tutti]
tr
[tutti]
[tutti]
[tutti]

II

38

25
solo
solo
solo
solo
29
tutti
tutti
tutti
tutti
[solo]
33
[solo]
[tutti]
[solo]
[solo]

III

Largo

6
[tutti]
[solo]
[tutti]
[solo]
[tutti]
p
f
p
f
12
tr
[solo]
18
[tutti]
[solo]
[tutti]

IV

14
[solo]
[solo]
[solo]
[solo]
18
[tutti]
[tutti]
[tutti]
[tutti]
22
p
p
p
p
[solo]
[solo]
[tutti]
[tutti]

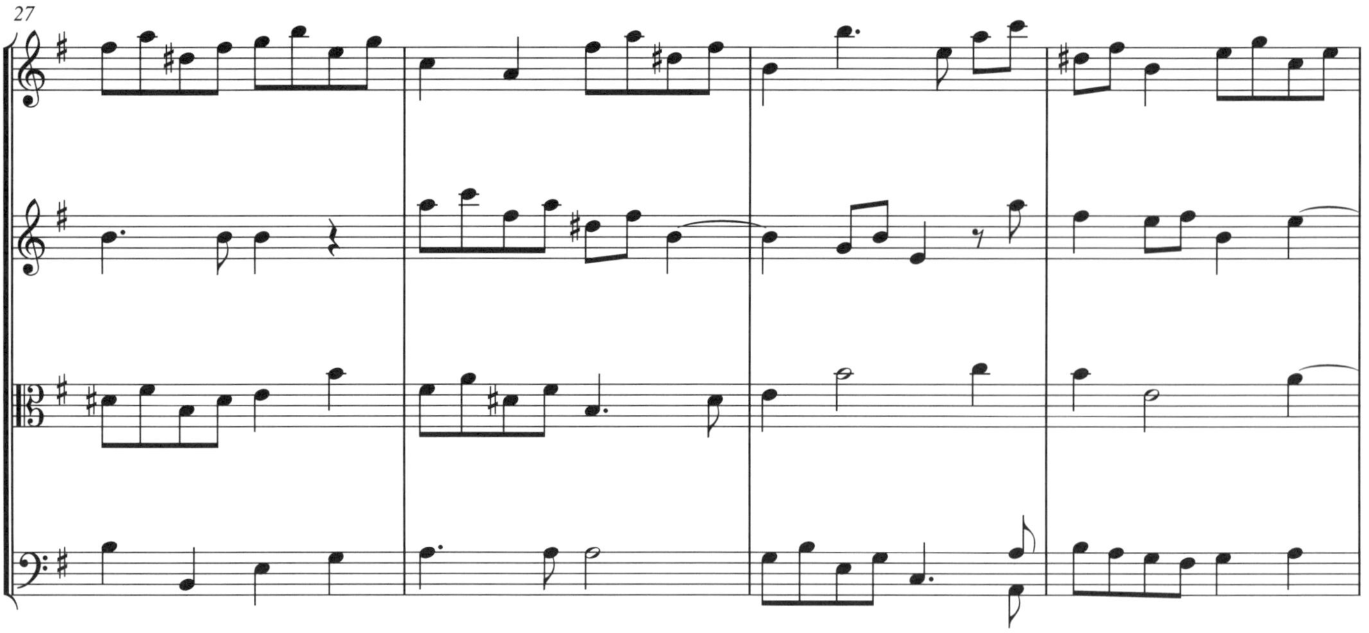
27

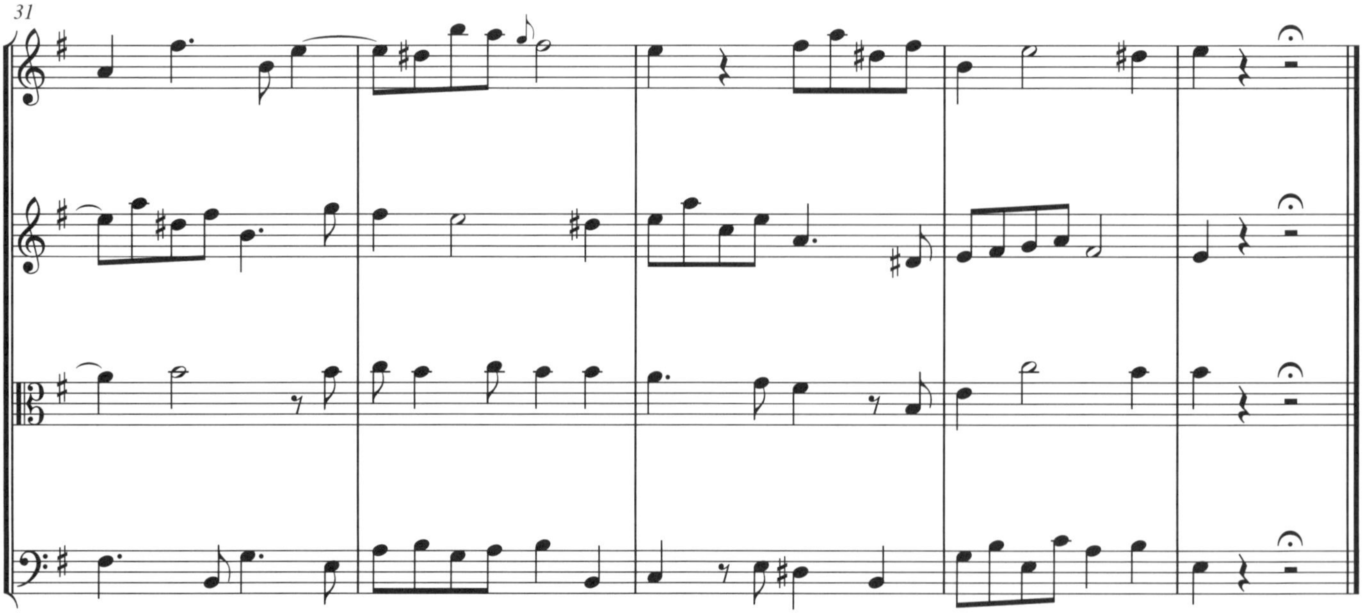
31

Concerto No. 8 in F Major

I

II

Largo

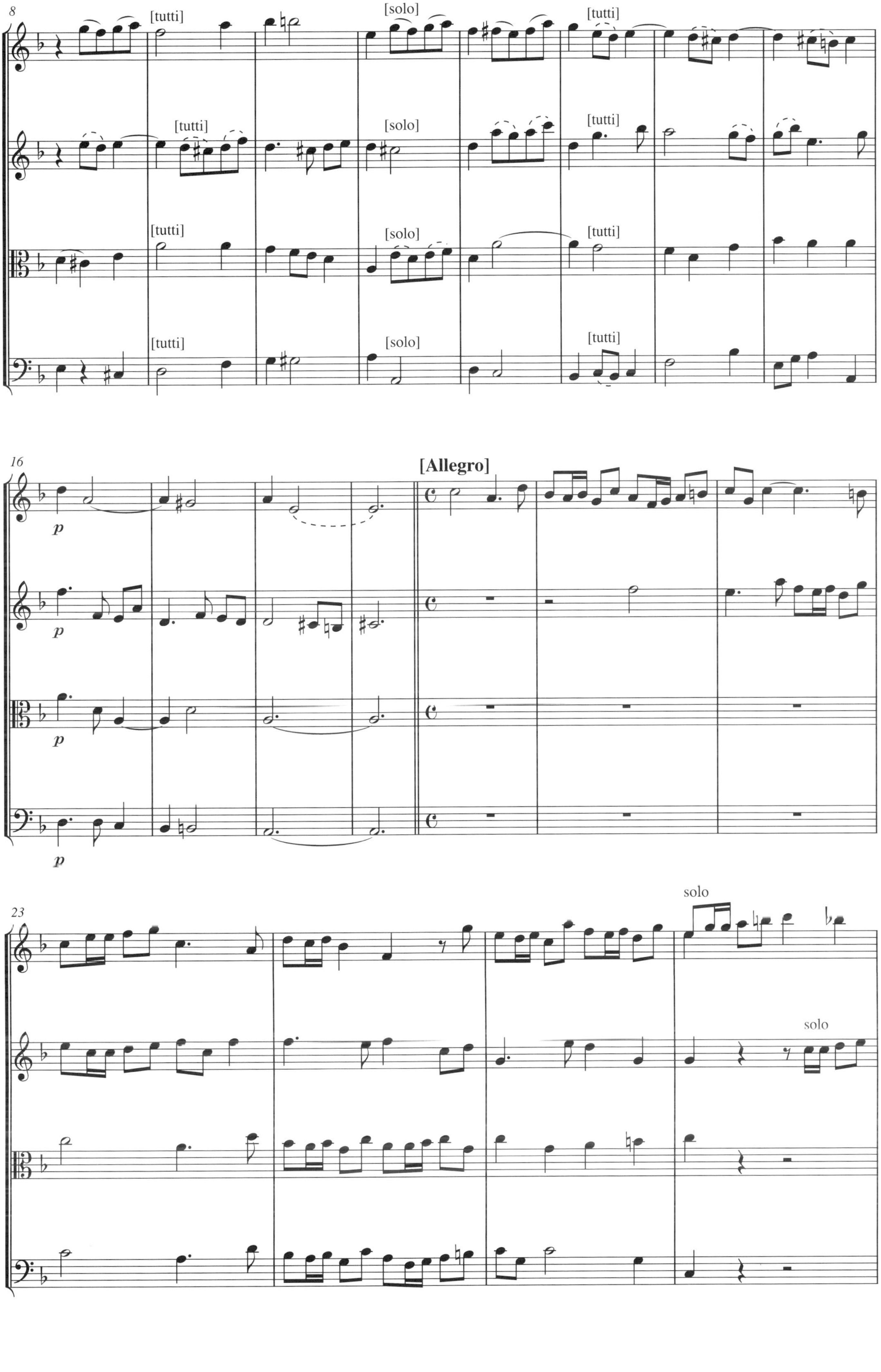
8
[tutti]
[solo]
[tutti]
16
[Allegro]
p
23
solo

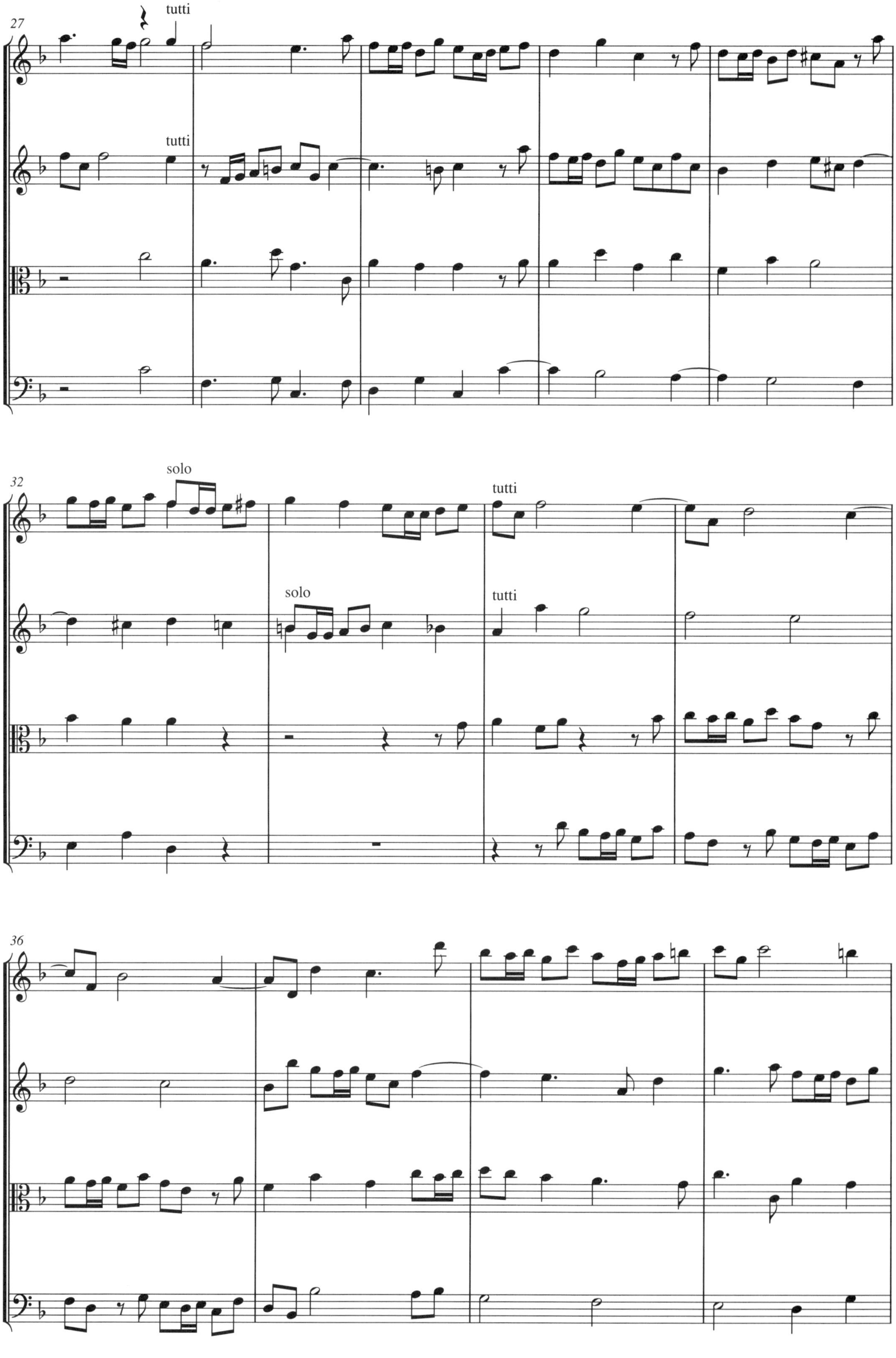
27
tutti
tutti
32
solo
solo
tutti
tutti
36

49

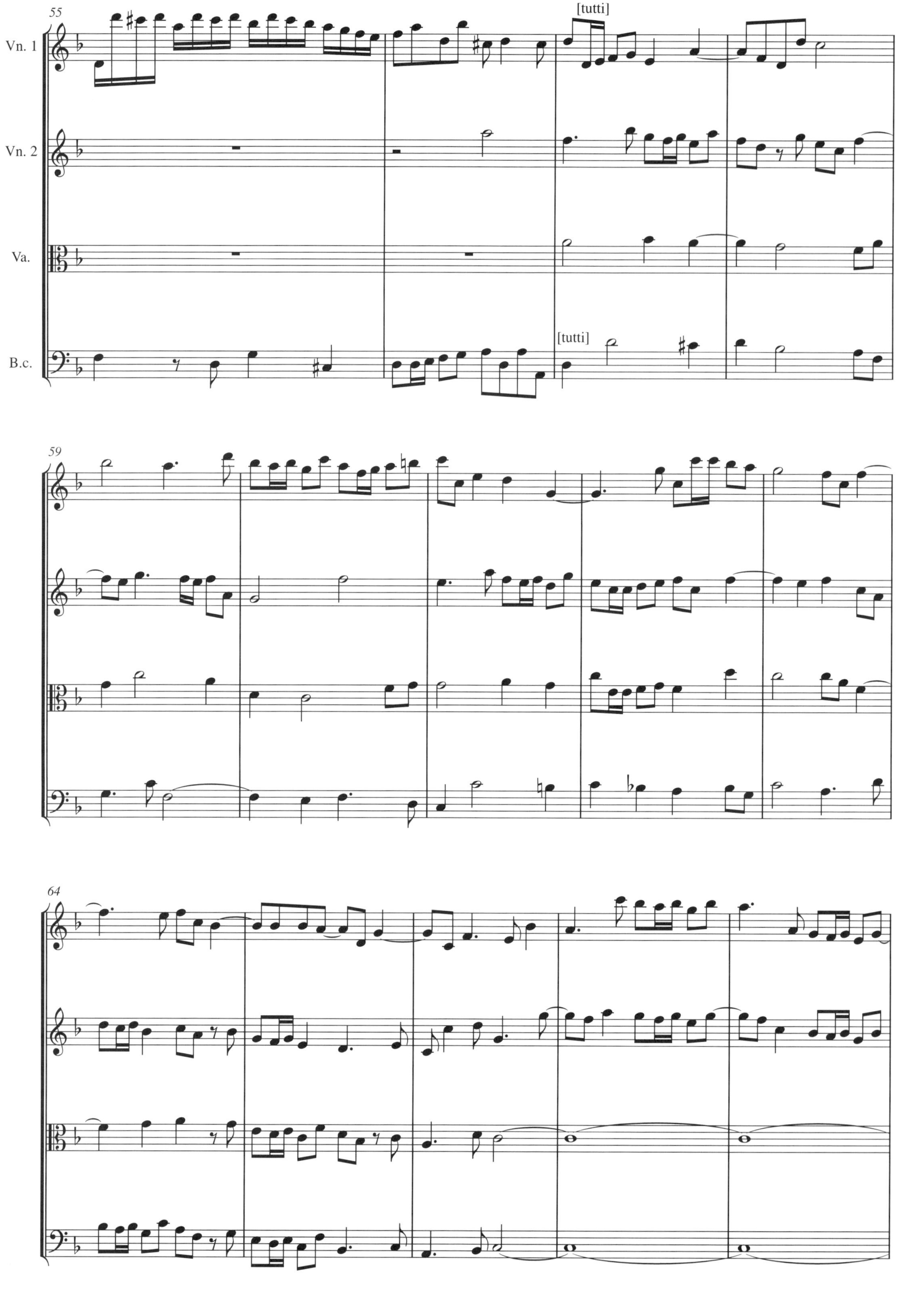
55
Vn. 1
Vn. 2
Va.
B.c.
[tutti]
[tutti]
59
64

III

Larghetto

11
[tutti]
[tutti]
[tutti]
[tutti]
17
[solo]
p
f
[solo]
p
f
tr
[solo]
p
f
[solo]
p
f
22
[tutti]
p
f
[solo]
[tutti]
p
f
[solo]
[tutti]
p
f
[solo]
[tutti]
p
f
[solo]

IV

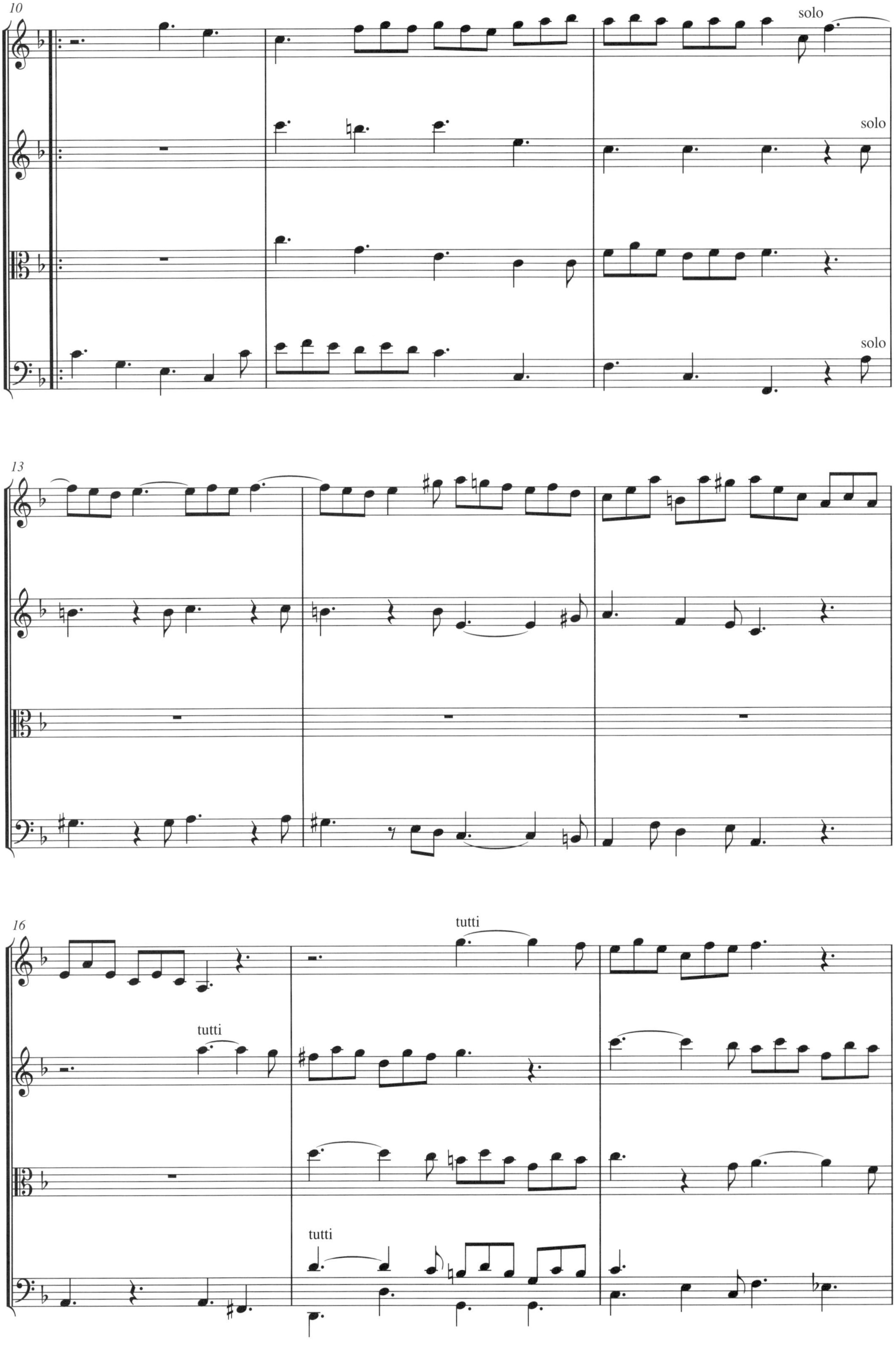
10
solo
solo
solo
13
16
tutti
tutti
tutti

55

56

Concerto No. 9 in D Major

I

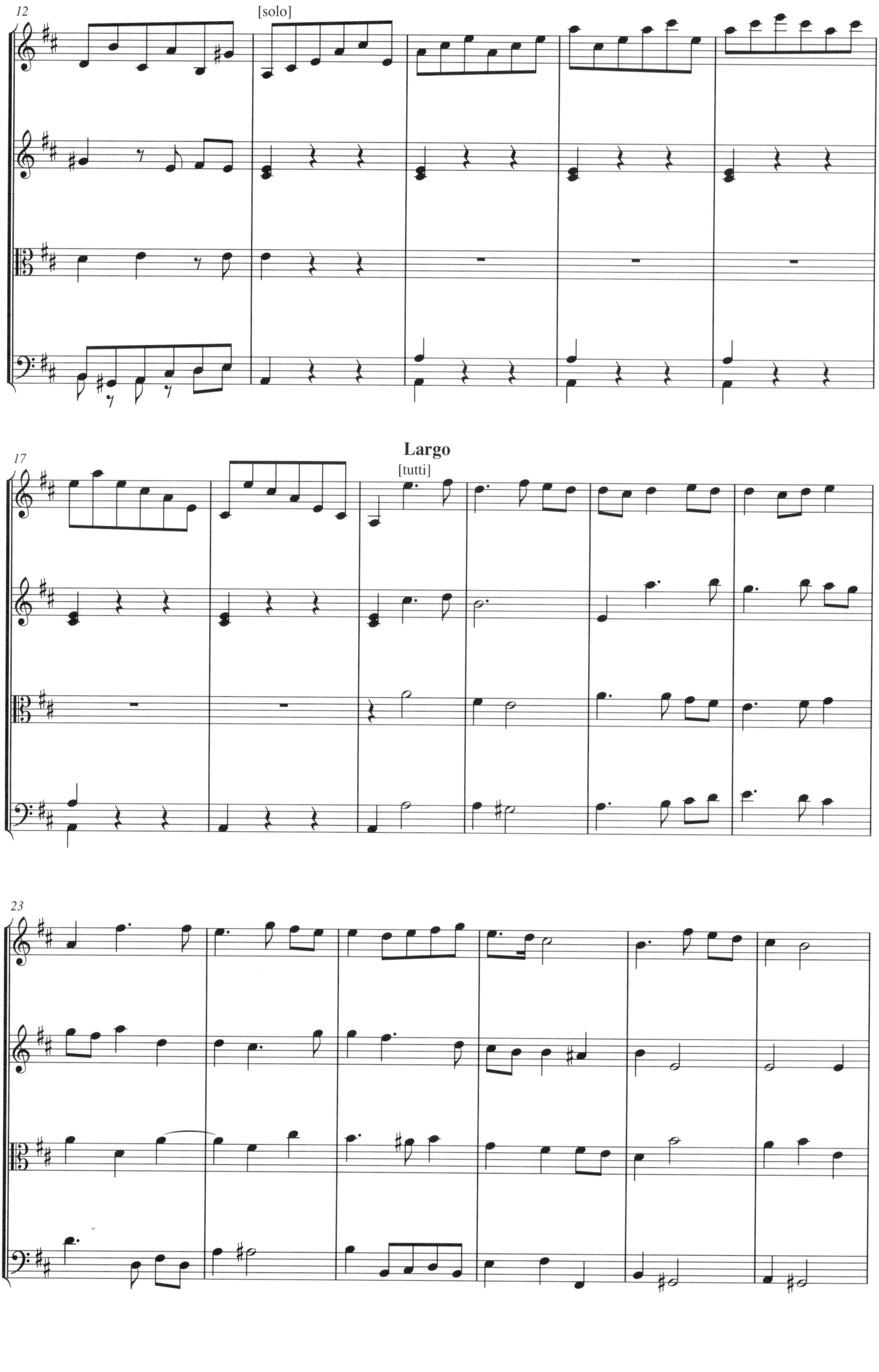
12
[solo]
17
Largo
[tutti]
23

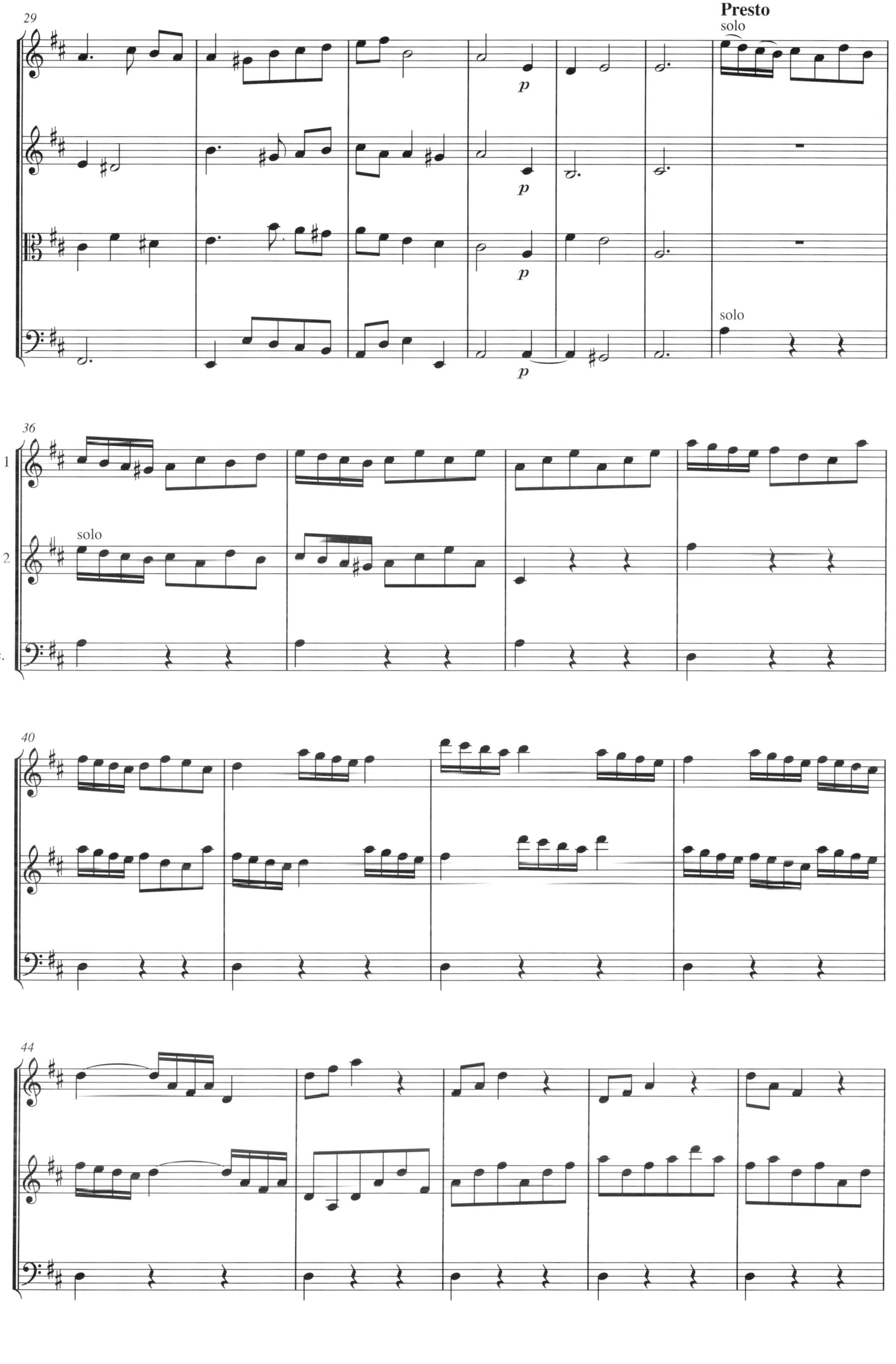
29
Presto
solo
p
p
p
p
solo
36
Vn. 1
solo
Vn. 2
B.c.
40
44

49
Largo
[tutti]
[solo]
[tutti]
Vn. 1
[tutti]
Vn. 2
Va.
[tutti]
B.c.
54
[solo]
[tutti]
59
p
f

II

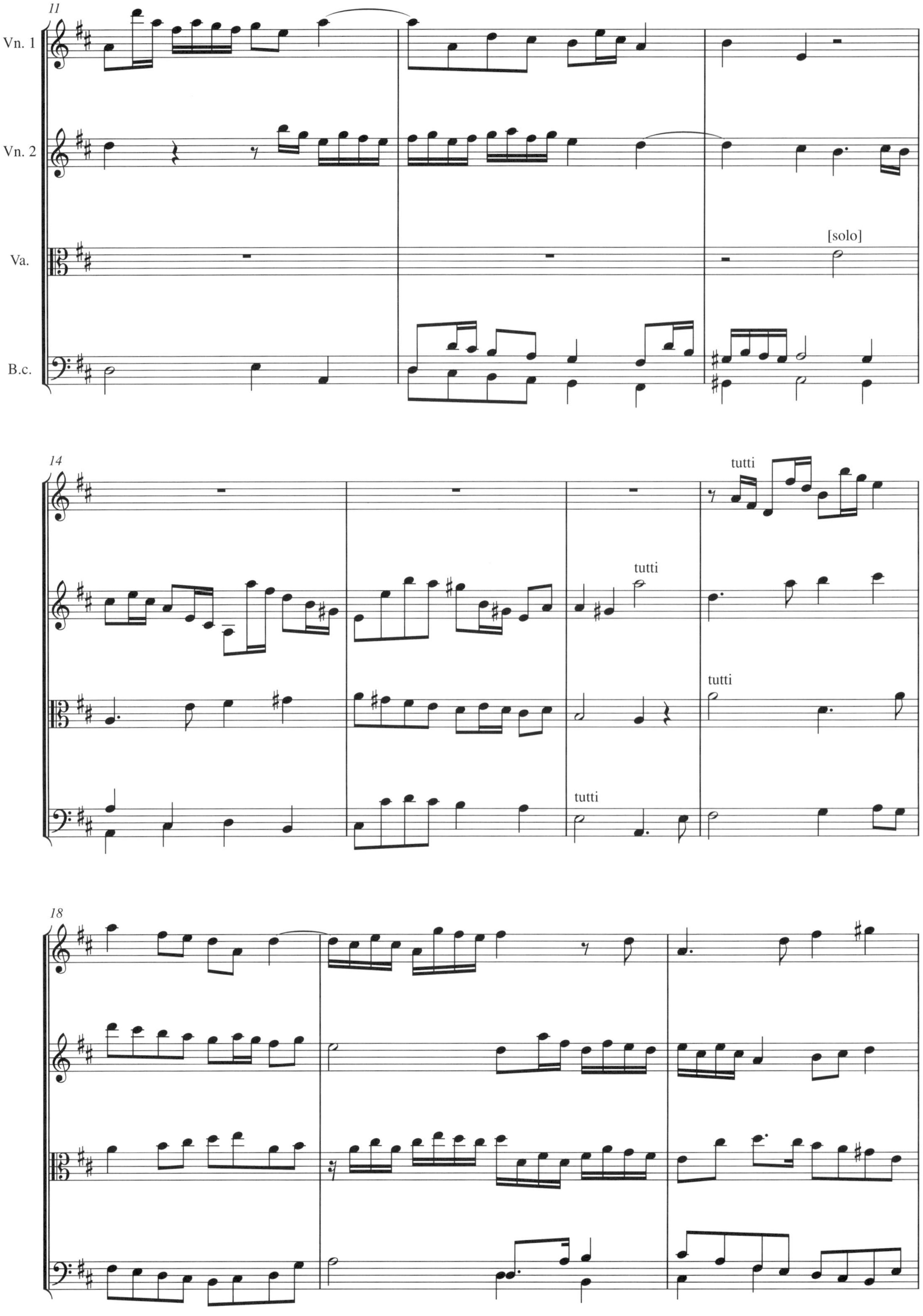
11
Vn. 1
Vn. 2
Va.
[solo]
B.c.
14
tutti
tutti
tutti
tutti
18

63

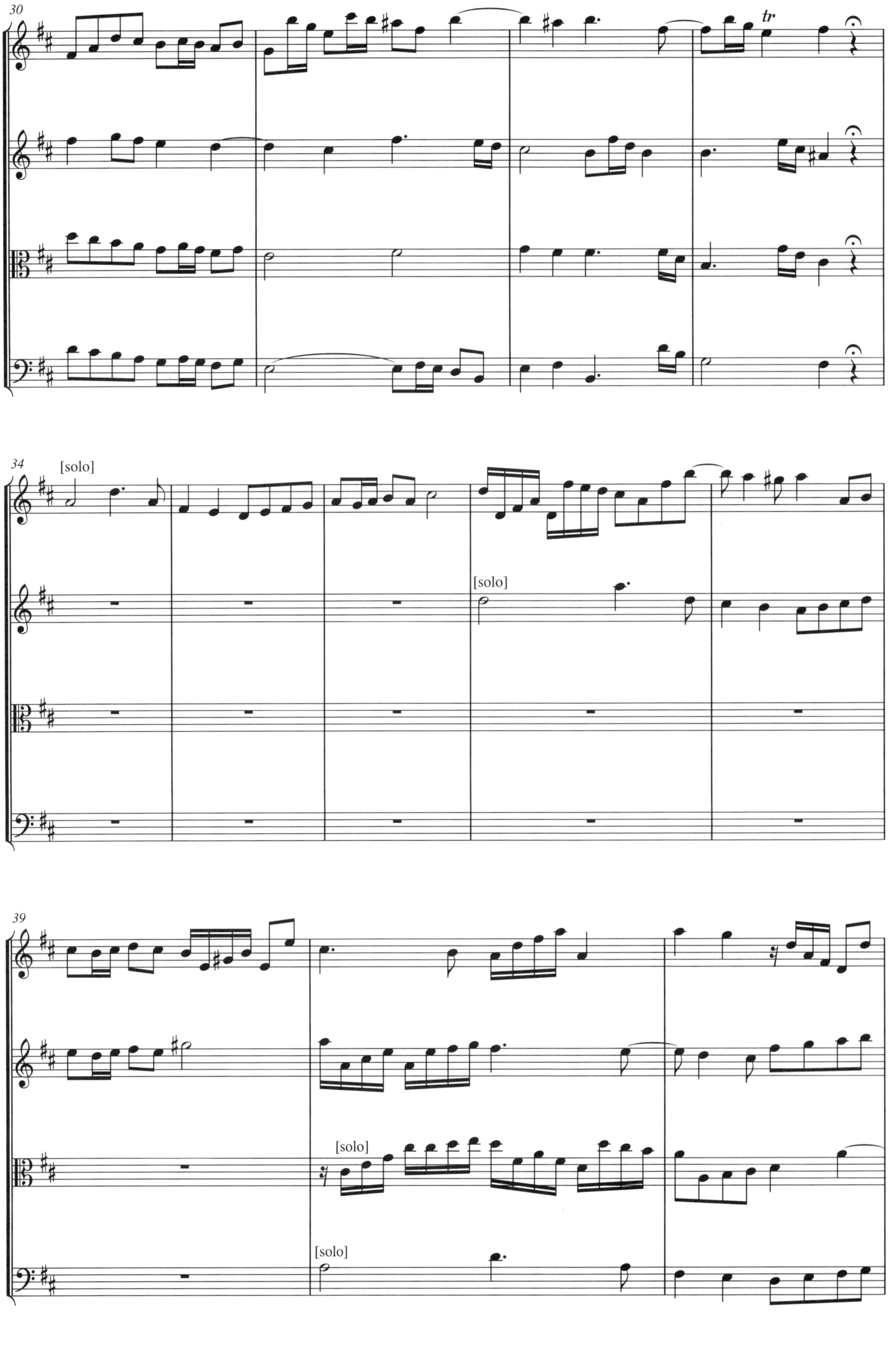
30
tr
34
[solo]
[solo]
39
[solo]
[solo]

65

III

Largo

7
[tutti]
[tutti]
[tutti]
[tutti]
13
[solo]
p
[tutti]
f
[solo]
p
[tutti]
f
f
[solo]
p
[tutti]
f
19

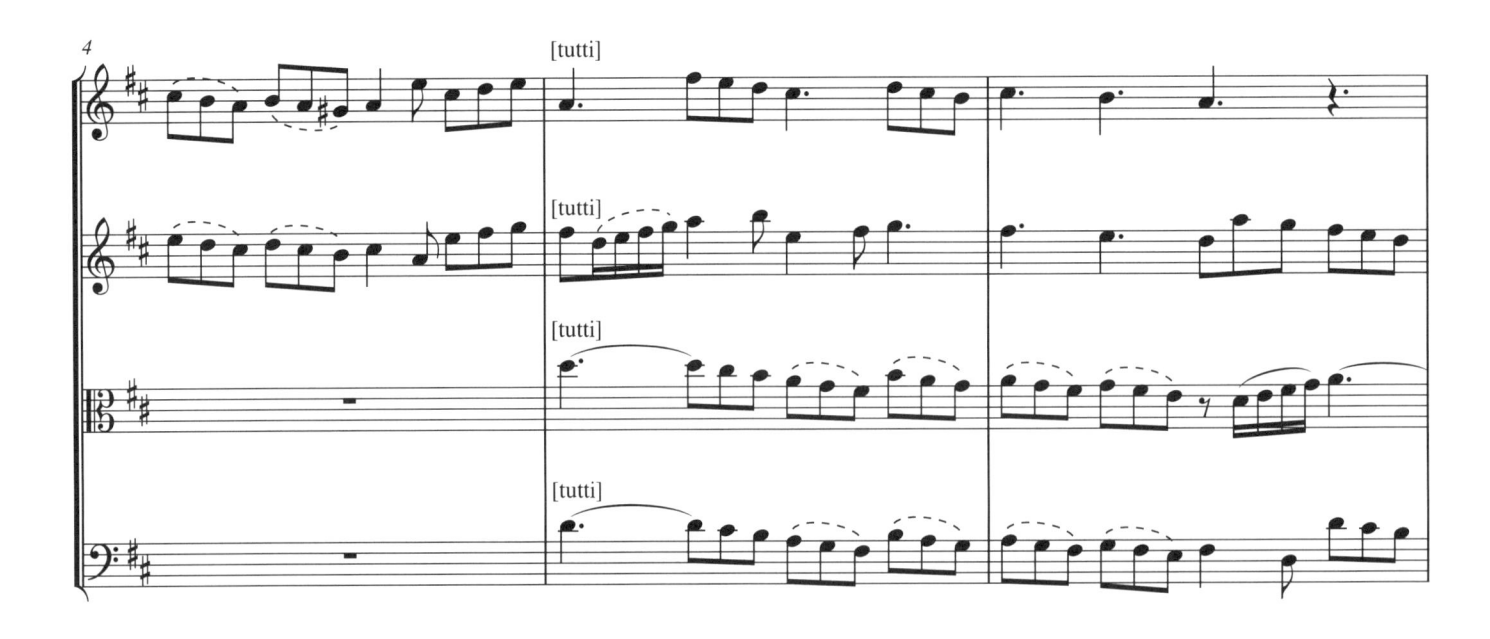

IV

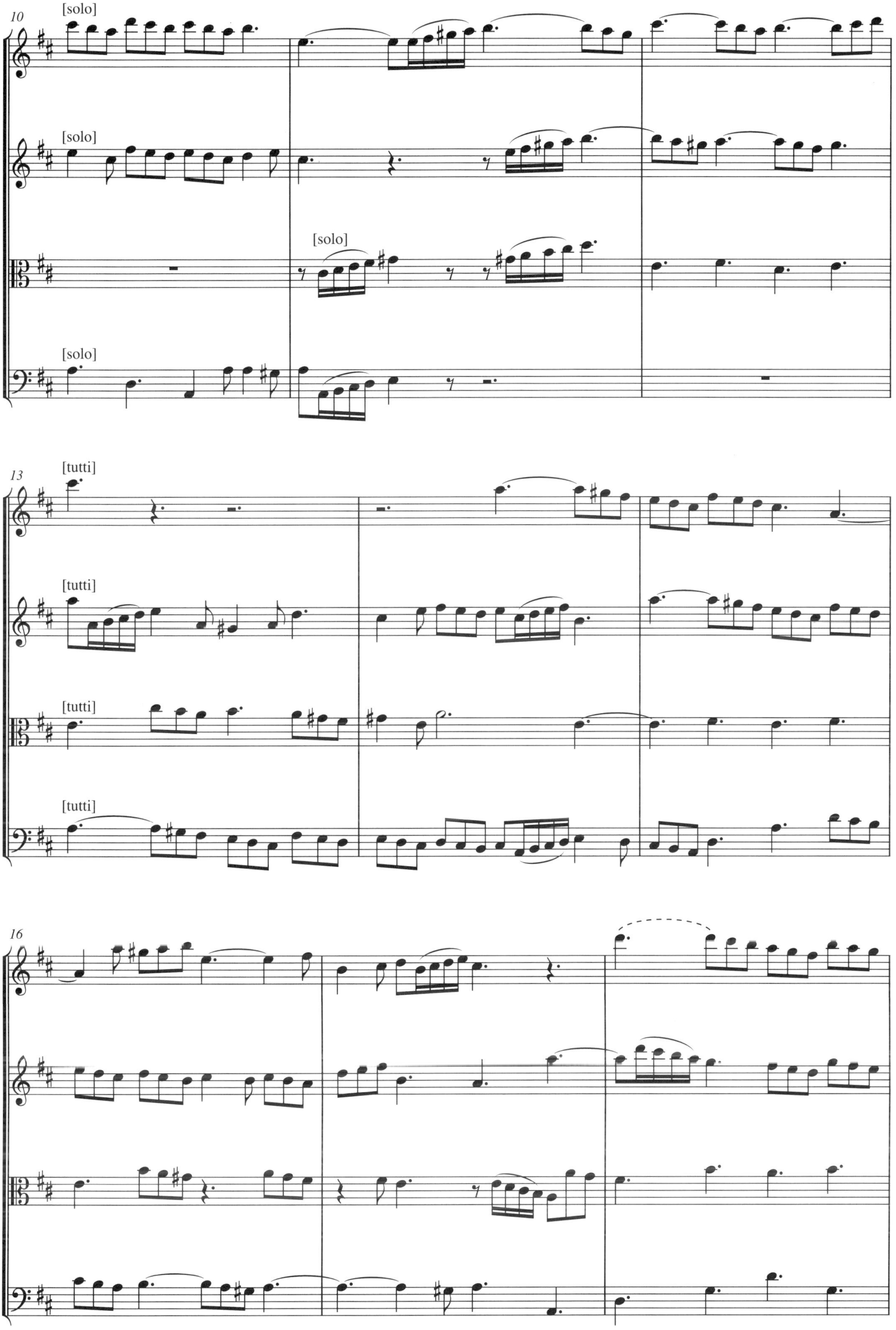
10
[solo]
[solo]
[solo]
[solo]
13
[tutti]
[tutti]
[tutti]
[tutti]
16

19
[solo]
[solo]
[solo]
[solo]
22
[tutti]
[tutti]
[tutti]
[tutti]
25
[solo]
[solo]
[solo]
[solo]

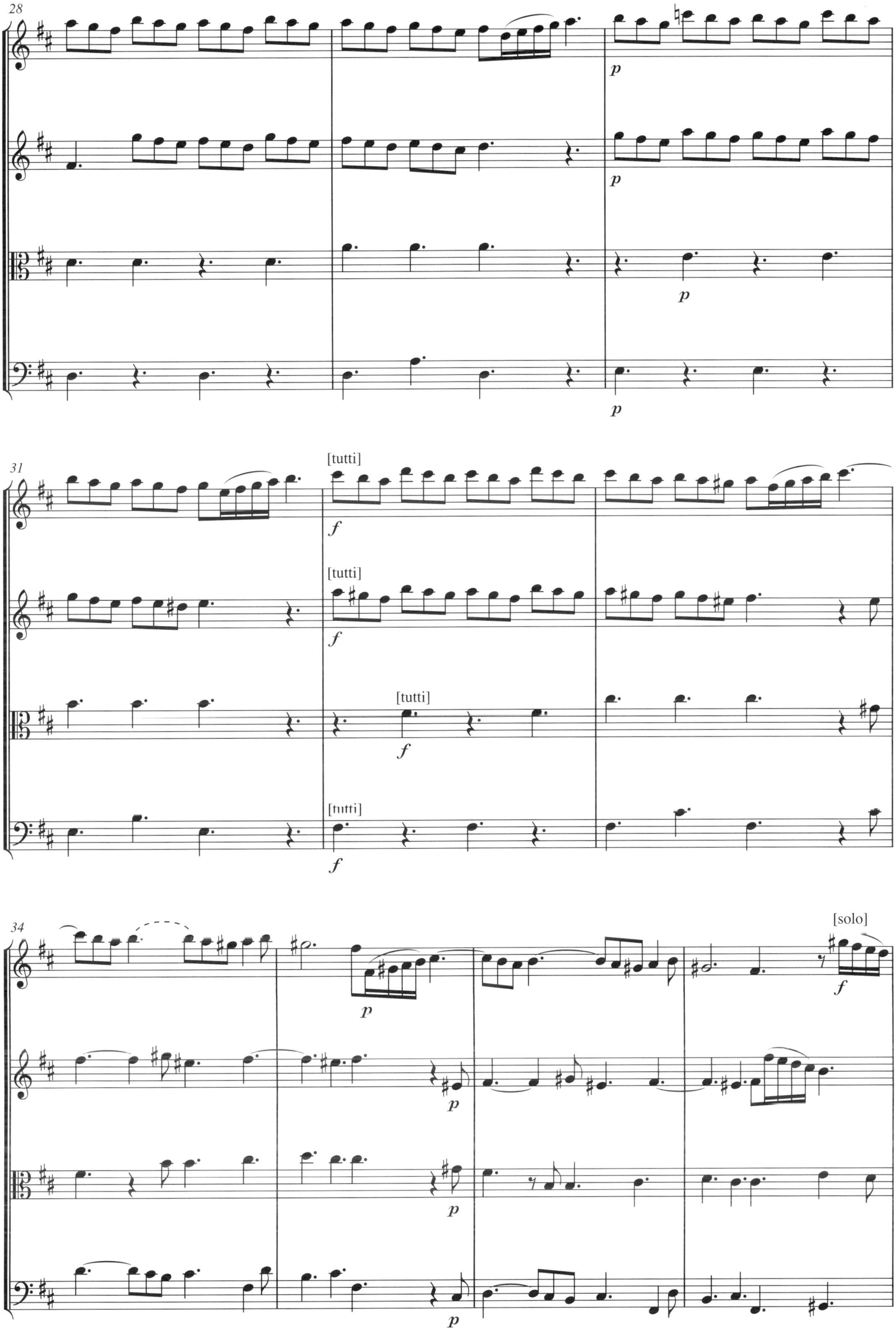
28
31
[tutti]
[tutti]
[tutti]
[tutti]
34
[solo]

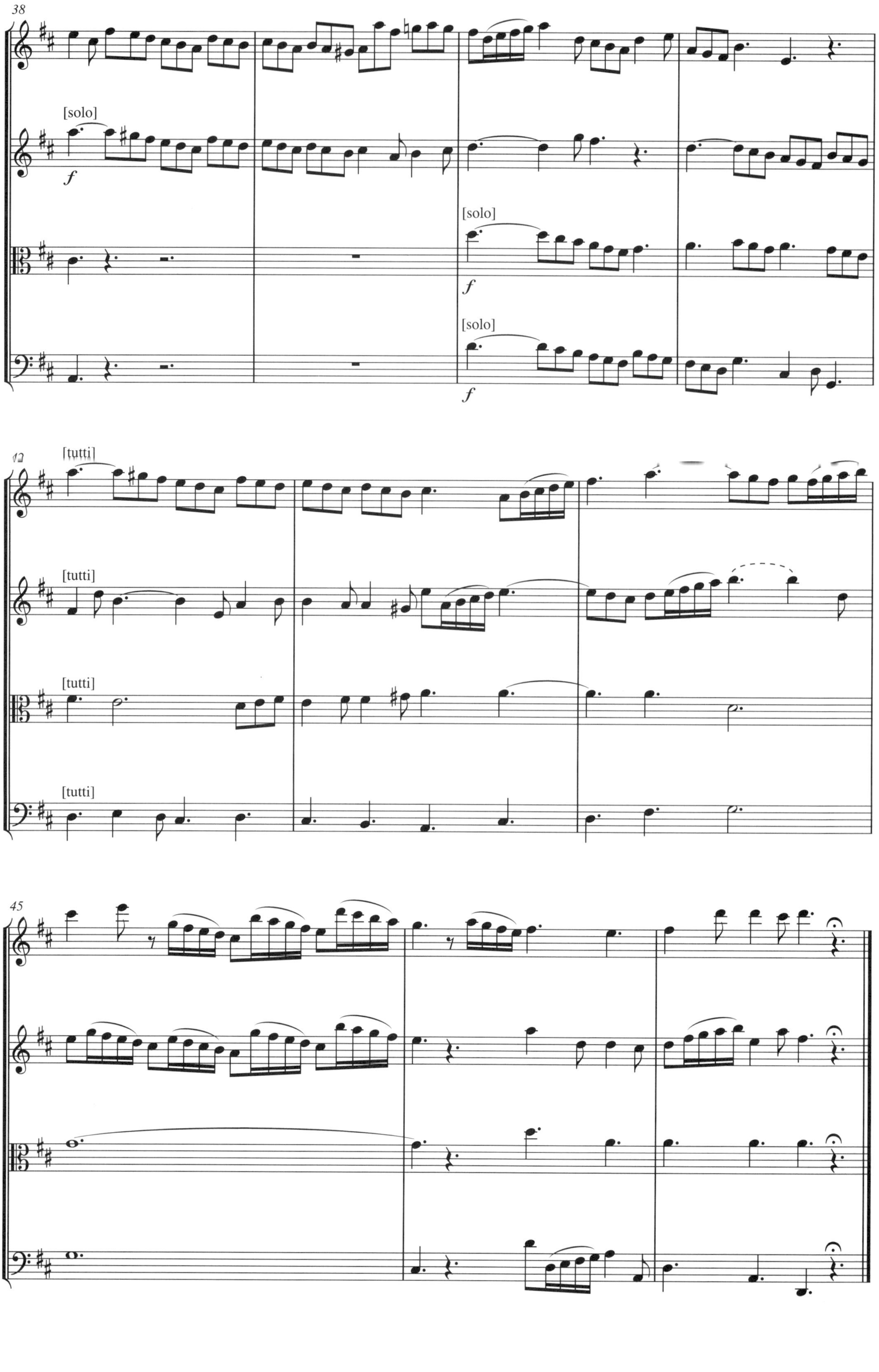
38
[solo]
f
[solo]
f
[solo]
f
[tutti]
[tutti]
[tutti]
[tutti]
45

Critical Report

Sources

There is only one source for the music of this edition: the first of two workbooks owned, used, and largely transcribed by the English composer Charles Avison (1709–70).[1] The two workbooks were discovered in 2000 and 2002 after being hidden from view for over two centuries. They are currently owned by the Charles Avison Society of Newcastle, England (i.e., the Avison Charitable Trust) and housed in the Charles Avison Archive, part of the larger Newcastle Collection at the Newcastle City Library. Workbook I consists of 276 pages in folio, and Workbook II has 328 pages. Watermark studies indicate that both books are of eighteenth-century manufacture and were probably first used between 1730 and 1740. At least five different hands can found in these workbooks, including those of Charles Avison and his son Edward (1747–76). Francesco Scarlatti's concerti grossi, however, are not in the hand of Charles or Edward, and the scribe cannot be positively identified. The concertos appear in Workbook I, folios 2r–27r.

Charles Avison, a pupil of Francesco Geminiani, was one of the leading advocates of the Italian concerto-grosso style in England during the eighteenth century.[2] He composed more than fifty works in the genre, among them his well-known concerto arrangements of Domenico Scarlatti's keyboard sonatas. Considering Avison's background and the popularity of the Italian style in England during his lifetime, it is not surprising that both workbooks contain a large number of works by Italian composers. In addition to the concertos of Francesco Scarlatti, Workbook I features music by a previously unknown member of the Scarlatti family, Stephani, as well as concertos by Geminiani, sonatas by Johann Adolph Hasse, and original compositions by Avison. Geminiani's music predominates in Workbook II, which also contains more works by Avison, including a few of his arrangements of Domenico Scarlatti's keyboard sonatas.

The six concertos of this edition are taken from a set of eleven "Sonatas" that are listed in the table of contents of Workbook I as "Eleven Sonata's [sic], 2 Violins, Viola & Bass." The table of contents, however, was probably added by Edward Avison late in the history of the workbooks, perhaps in 1776. The term "sonata" also appears at the top of the page of the first concerto (see plate 1), where the heading "Sonate da Sigr. Francesco Scarlatti" is written before the first piece, and in a hand different from that of Edward Avison. The six concertos of this edition were chosen from the complete set of eleven because they are the strongest musically and best represent Scarlatti's compositional style in this genre.

Editorial Methods

Whether Scarlatti always used the term "sonata" to imply a concerto grosso is impossible to tell with certainty, since the compositions in Workbook I are his only known works in this genre. Moreover, the source labels individual works simply with numbers, without the descriptive title of "sonata." Nevertheless, despite the use of "sonata" in the source, a number of factors indicate that these works were intended to be performed by a string ensemble as concerti grossi: the instrumentation listed in the table of contents, the use of four-part open score for all the compositions, and the appearance of the words "solo" and "tutti" and double stems at various points throughout each work. This edition therefore adds without brackets the title "concerto" for each piece and includes the number that appears in the source; the piece numbered "1" in the source is given the editorial title "Concerto No. 1 in E Major;" what is "2" in the source has the editorial title "Concerto No. 2 in C Minor," and so forth. Roman numerals are added without brackets to designate movements.

The use of barlines to indicate the end of a section, movement, and concerto is inconsistent in the source and differs from modern practices. The end of a concerto, for example, is marked with a single barline followed by a wavy line (see plate 4); this edition converts these single barlines to a final (thin-thick) barline. The source uses thin-thin barlines to indicate both the end of a movement and the end of a section within a multitempo movement, making it difficult at times to determine whether a portion of music qualifies as an independent movement. In most cases, the end of a movement is followed by blank staves, and the next movement begins on the following page (see plates 1, 2, and 3). Divisions within movements are also usually shown with thin-thin barlines, but normal barlines—or, in a few places, no barlines at all—appear in places in which the tempo changes abruptly (e.g., Concerto No. 9, I). Regardless of whether the situation calls for a single or double barline, however, the next section begins without any intervening empty staves. For this edition, thin-thin barlines at the ends of movements have been converted to final (thin-thick) barlines. Thin-thin barlines in the source indicating divisions within movements have been retained, as has the use of normal barlines for those places in which the tempo changes without a clear section break. As the source is not always consistent in the use of empty staves, other musical features—including the presence of fermatas or the length of a particular section—have also been used to determine whether a particular section of music should be considered an independent movement. Places in which a movement ends without being followed by empty staves are reported in the critical notes.

As the source does not list the instruments at the beginning of each concerto, this edition adds instrument names tacitly in conformity with the standard concerto-grosso ensemble of the period. Original clefs are retained, including the occasional use of tenor clef in the bass line, which often implies passages played only by the cello, without double bass. (Passages marked "solo" are similarly to be played only by the cello; see "Notes on Performance" in the introduction.) A harpsichord was certainly part of the ensemble in these concertos, as it was in all works in the genre from this period. This is further confirmed by Scarlatti's use of figures and the words "tasto solo" at various points in the concertos.

The source's system of notating passages to be played by the *concertino* or *ripieno* sections is often difficult to interpret in these works, as the *concertino* and *ripieno* sections share the same staves on a four-staff system. (Avison's customary format is to use seven staves and keep the *concertino* and *ripieno* sections separate.) The source sometimes has the terms "solo" or "tutti," uses double stems, or adds musical material to certain instrumental parts for this purpose, but the placement and meaning of these notational devices are far from consistent or clear. This edition retains the written solo and tutti indications of the original. If the source used a double stem to indicate the beginning of a tutti passage, the edition tacitly deletes the stem and replaces it with a tutti directive. When a solo or tutti designation appears in only one part, the designation is tacitly added to the remaining parts. Stems and, on occasion, the abbreviations "conc." and "rip." are tacitly added to clarify places in which *concertino* and *ripieno* overlap. In such instances, the *concertino* part is notated with upward stems, *ripieno* with downward stems. This edition adds editorial suggestions in brackets to clarify further the distribution of *concertino* and *ripieno*, basing decisions on an analysis of each work and comparisons with concertos by other composers that are more clearly notated. Passages that are especially virtuosic, for example, have been labeled solo, as have the initial subject entries of most fugal movements. If a movement lacks an opening solo or tutti indication in the source but has a directive later in the movement, the opposite directive was added retroactively to the movement's opening. However, since it is impossible to determine all the divisions of *concertino* and *ripieno* with absolute certainty, performers are encouraged to make further interpretations in this regard. The abbreviation "div." appears in brackets to clarify divisi passages within *ripieno* sections.

Original time and key signatures are retained, as are original note values. Notes that appear tied within a measure in the source have been tacitly realized as a single note of comparable duration wherever viable in the edition, particularly in those movements in which the source is inconsistent in the use of tied notes. The stem directions, beaming patterns, and rhythmic groupings of notes and rests in the source are made to conform to modern conventions in the edition. Particularly in the staff shared by cello and double bass, stems have tacitly been adjusted to clarify notation. The notation of appoggiaturas is retained from the source, that is, with stems up and without slurs underneath. Triplet numerals are placed at the beam or stem side of notes, as they are found in the source.

All editorially added accidentals are placed in brackets. Added cautionary accidentals are placed in parentheses; source cautionaries are retained only where they clarify passages. Accidentals of the source that are redundant by modern standards are tacitly removed. Due to space limitations, accidentals in the source frequently appear above notes; other accidentals appear next to notes with little regard to precise position on the correct line or space (see plate 1). In both of these cases, accidentals are corrected and moved to the left of the note without comment. Obvious errors in pitches and rhythm are corrected and indicated in the critical notes. Either because of scribal mistakes or other factors, a number of instances of incorrect voice leading or serious harmonic clashes appear in the source. These errors have been corrected in conformity with the harmonic and contrapuntal practices of the period, at least as much as possible without completely recomposing certain passages, and indicated in the critical notes. Only a few measures are provided with a figured bass in the source. These figures are retained in the edition, with the exception that slashed numerals (such as 6) are rendered in the edition with a ♯ or ♮ before the numeral, and accidentals are moved to appear before figures (such as ♭6 rather than 6♭). Except for a single editorial figure, shown in brackets in the Concerto No. 2 in C Minor, no attempt is made to add additional figures. Nonetheless, the bass is to be fully realized.

Tempo and other written directives are placed above the top staff. Tempo markings are not provided for every movement in the original; editorially added tempos appear in brackets. Fermatas do not always appear consistently in all four parts in the source; when they appear in only one part, they are tacitly realized in the remaining parts. The source contains few dynamic markings; those that do appear in the source typically appear in only one part and are written out in full ("piano" or "forte"). Original dynamics are retained, tacitly converted to modern abbreviations, and realized in all four parts. Editorially added dynamics appear in bold roman typeface.

The source features only one ornament sign: a trill. Editorial trills appear in brackets. Source markings that imply a staccato or accented note are not consistent. The majority of such signs, however, are thin strokes. These have been retained, and additional strokes are added in parentheses in parallel passages. We do not have any concrete information about the proper performance of these strokes for the works of Francesco Scarlatti. It is probably safe to assume that they indicate a shortening of the notes, much like the modern staccato. Editorial ties and slurs are dashed. The source contains relatively few slurs, and editorially added slurs have largely been limited to two scenarios: (1) subsequent entries of a fugue theme; and (2) moments in which two parts move in parallel, but only one part has been marked with slurs in the source. When a motive repeats numerous times and is shown with articulation slurs the first few times, however, editorial slurs are not added to every repetition. Rather, performers should understand that the first slurs set up a pattern that should persist throughout the passage. The only exception to this system is the fourth movement of Concerto No. 2, in which the source is particularly inconsistent with regard to slur placement. In this case, editorial slurs are limited to a handful of fugue entries. Performers are encouraged to pay especially close attention to other possible places in which to add slurs.

Critical Notes

Critical notes list rejected or ambiguous readings from the source. Notes are located in the score by measure number and part name. When specific notes and rests in a measure are cited, appoggiaturas are included in the note count, tied noteheads are numbered individually, and rests are counted separately from notes. The following abbreviations are used in the paragraphs below: M(m.) = measure(s), Vn. = violin, Va. = viola, B.c. = basso continuo. The pitch system used throughout is that in which c' represents middle C.

Concerto No. 1 in E Major

I. ALLEGRO

M. 6, Vn. 2, note 4, double stem. M. 7, Vn. 2, note 7, double stem. M. 10, Vn. 1, note 9, double stem. M. 12, B.c., note 4 is f♯. M. 19, Va., note 2 is f♯' quarter note with double stem.

II. [ALLEGRO]

M. 21, Va., notes 5–7 are e"–d"–c♯". M. 22, Va., note 1 is b♯'. M. 31, B.c., note 3, double stem.

III. LARGO; [ALLEGRO]

M. 1, Tempo illegible, possibly "Largo e puntelo." M. 16, Va., notes 2–3 are d'–d'.

IV. AFFETTUOSO

M. 16, Vn. 1, notes 3–6 are 8th, 16th, and two 32nd notes. M. 58, Vn. 1, note 3 is 16th note. M. 59, Vn. 1, slur over notes 2–4.

Concerto No. 2 in C Minor

II. ANDANTE

M. 11, Vn. 1, note 2 is d".

III. GRAVE

Movement follows immediately after double barline of Andante without intervening blank staves.

Concerto No. 3 in A Minor

III. [LARGHETTO]

M. 4, Va., beat 3, extra half note a'.

IV. [ALLEGRO]

M. 18, Vn. 1, notes 4 and 5, thin strokes above notes. M. 19, Vn. 1, note 2 is dotted quarter note. M. 31, B.c., beat 4, extra G♯ quarter note above E.

Concerto No. 4 in E Minor

II. ALLEGRO

M. 6, Vn. 1, note 4, f♯" appears above d". M. 9, Va., beat 3 is quarter note and 8th rest. M. 24, Va., beat 3, b appears above 8th rest. M. 43, Vn. 1, beats 2 and 3 have tied quarter notes with thin strokes.

III. LARGO

Movement follows immediately after double barline of Allegro without intervening blank staves. M. 4, Va., note 1 is g'. M. 13, Vn. 1, note 1, b appears below f♯'. M. 15, Va., beat 1 is g' quarter note. M. 19, B.c., beats 2 and 3 are e'–f♯'–e'–f♯'. M. 20, B.c., beats 1 and 2 are e'–e.

IV. [ALLEGRO]

M. 5, B.c., note 2, c appears above A. M. 15, B.c., beat 4 has two 8th notes b–c♯. M. 16, B.c., beat 3, extra quarter note e.

Concerto No. 8 in F Major

II. LARGO; [ALLEGRO]

Mm. 18–19, barline lacking. M. 34, Va., note 2 is g'. M. 62, B.c., note 5 is f. M. 71, Vn. 2, note 8 is b'.

III. LARGHETTO

M. 1, two tempo indications: Larghetto and Largo. M. 9, word "below" written between staves of Vn. 1 and Vn. 2.

IV. ALLEGRO

Movement follows immediately after double barline of Larghetto without intervening empty staves. M. 71, Vn. 2, note 8 is b♭'.

Concerto No. 9 in D Major

I. GRAVE; PRESTO; LARGO; PRESTO; LARGO

M. 9, Vn. 1, note 2, double stem is quarter note. M. 60, beat 1, *p* (moved to m. 59, beat 3). M. 62, Va., note 2 is quarter note and 8th rest.

II. Larghetto

M. 6, Vn. 1, ♯ on note 7, rather than on note 4.   M. 34, illegible word between staves of Vn. 1 and Vn. 2, possibly indicating the introduction of the fugue theme in inversion.   M. 40, Va., notes 5–7 are a′–b′–c♯″.

IV. Presto

Movement begins immediately after double barline of Largo without intervening empty staves.

Notes

1. With more than six hundred pages of music and text, the two workbooks offer new perspectives on Avison and his role in the development of the orchestral concerto in the eighteenth century. For further information, including the dramatic events leading to the discovery of the workbooks, see Mark Kroll, "Two Important New Sources for the Music of Charles Avison," *Music and Letters* 86 (2005): 414–31.

2. Information about Avison's life and works can be found in Jenny Burchell, *Polite or Commercial Concerts? Concert Management and Orchestral Repertoire in Edinburgh, Bath, Oxford, Manchester and Newcastle, 1730–1799* (New York: Garland, 1996); Pierre Dubois, ed., *Charles Avison's Essay on Musical Expression* (Aldershot: Ashgate, 2004); P. M. Horsley, "Charles Avison: The Man and His Milieu," *Music and Letters* 51 (1974): 5–23; Roz Southey, *Music-Making in North-East England During the Eighteenth Century* (Aldershot: Ashgate, 2006); Norris Lynn Stephens, "Charles Avison: An Eighteenth-Century English Composer, Musician and Writer" (Ph.D. diss., University of Pittsburgh, 1968); and my edition of Charles Avison, *Concerto Grosso Arrangements of Geminiani's Opus 1 Violin Sonatas*, Recent Researches in the Music of the Baroque Era, vol. 160 (Middleton, Wis.: A-R Editions, 2010).